D1637768

Re.

HITLER'S
LAST DAYS

AN EYE-WITNESS ACCOUNT

About the author

GERHARD BOLDT was trained as a cavalry officer, having been rejected for the normal infantry training and dismissed from the Hitler Youth movement for insubordination. During the war he served on both Western and Eastern Fronts and was twice decorated. At the very end of the war he worked with Reinhard Gehlen on military intelligence concerning the Eastern Front and was thus able to record at first-hand the last days of Hitler and the Third Reich. He himself escaped from Berlin and returned with his family to Lubeck, his home town, where he had a wines and spirits business. He was closely concerned as a technical adviser with the making of the film. *Hitler: The Last Ten Days*, in which Sir Alec Guinness plays the title role. Boldt's book was one of the major sources for the film.

HITLER'S
LAST DAYS

AN EYE-WITNESS ACCOUNT

GERHARD BOLDT

Translated by Sandra Bance

PEN & SWORD MILITARY CLASSICS

First published in Germany in 1947 by Rowohlt Verlag GmbH
under the title *Die letzten Tage der Reichskanzlei;*
revised German edition (paperback) published in 1964.

New English edition first published in Great Britain by Arthur Barker Ltd 1973.

Published in this format in 2005 by
Pen & Sword Military Classics
An imprint of
Pen & Sword Books Ltd
47 Church Street
Barnsley
South Yorkshire
S70 2AS

Copyright © Gerhard Boldt, 1947, 1964, 1973, 2005
English translation © Arthur Barker Ltd 1973, 2005

ISBN 1 84415 361 4

The right of Gerhard Boldt to be identified as Author of this work has been asserted
by him in accordance with the Copyright, Designs and Patents Act 1988.

A CIP catalogue record for this book is
available from the British Library

Printed and bound in England
By CPI UK

Pen & Sword Books Ltd incorporates the Imprints of Pen & Sword Aviation,
Pen & Sword Maritime, Pen & Sword Military, Wharncliffe Local history,
Pen & Sword Select, Pen & Sword Military Classics and Leo Cooper.

For a complete list of Pen & Sword titles please contact
PEN & SWORD BOOKS LIMITED
47 Church Street, Barnsley, South Yorkshire, S70 2AS, England
E-mail: enquiries@pen-and-sword.co.uk
Website: www.pen-and-sword.co.uk

Contents

Illustrations

Allied soldiers mopping up resistance (*Mansell Collection*)
The remains of the great table in the Chancellery
  (*Ullstein*)
The Nazi eagle fallen (*Imperial War Museum*)
Women soldiers in Berlin (*Wiener Library*)
The trench in the Reich Chancellery gardens (*Ullstein*)

The author and publishers would like to thank the Imperial War Museum, the Mansell Collection, the Wiener Library, Ullstein Bilderdienst and the Zeitgeschichtliches Bildarchiv Heinrich Hoffmann for their permission to reproduce the photographs from their collections. Those photographs not specifically acknowledged are from the author's own collection.

INTRODUCTION

The cheerlessness of a wet and chilly winter's day lay over the countryside. It was February 1945. A few minutes before on this drive north we had passed the gates and sentries of Maybach I and Maybach II, the headquarters of the Armed Forces. I sat next to the driver of the grey Mercedes; behind me sat General Heinz Guderian (Chief of German General Staff since 20 July 1944) and his adjutant Major Bernd von Freytag-Loringhoven. Nobody was talking. We all had many things on our minds to keep us silent and preoccupied, particularly Guderian.

In the course of the last three weeks of war, the Russian armies had pushed forward to the Oder. Seventy kilometres from the gates of Berlin they had crossed the river and established bridgeheads on its western bank. The German High Command had no more reserves to throw into the battle against this dire threat to the capital. Unless for some strange reason the Russian armies under Marshal Grigori Zhukov decided of their own accord to give up their headlong advance, Berlin's fate would very soon be sealed.

After about two weeks as chief aide to the head of the German General Staff, on this particular day I was to accompany Guderian to the Reich Chancellery for a situation conference with the Supreme Commander of the German Armed Forces, Adolf Hitler. I was to be presented to the Führer and, in case I should ever need to substitute for Freytag-Loringhoven, initiated into the duties of an adjutant to Guderian.

Perhaps it was because I had so recently left a different world, the world of a family party in Lübeck for my twenty-seventh birthday, or perhaps it was because I was so aware of the novelty and unfamiliarity of what lay ahead – whatever the reason, on this drive towards Hitler and the Reich Chancellery, I found myself passing in review the events that had led me to this point.

Lübeck was once a province of the German Empire. It forfeited its autonomy in 1937 when, under Nazi rule, it was annexed by Prussia. The city and its municipality, formerly a town of the Hanseatic League, is situated on the lower reaches of the Trave. Churches, gabled town-houses, merchant halls and old fortifications testify to a proud and tradition-conscious past. I was born here in 1918 and I grew up in a well-to-do family, surrounded by an atmosphere of middle-class security. An interest in music, good books, rowing and riding characterized my early years.

A sudden upheaval burst in upon this cloistered existence when Hitler became Chancellor in 1933 and seized power for his National Socialist German Workers' Party. That year I became a member of the Hitler Youth, the political organization for boys between the ages of fifteen and eighteen. As a result of this a first whiff of politics was blown into my life. Perhaps it was the sense of doing something new and the accent on sports and games, or perhaps it was the clear-cut goals and the consciously created examples which attracted me to the Hitler Youth. I certainly enjoyed the new spirit of comradeship, investing it with a great deal of youthful idealism, and was soon made the leader of my youth group. But this was not to last for long. I had been brought up to have an opinion of my own and to speak my mind. It was precisely this which brought me into conflict with the leadership of the local Hitler Youth and in 1936 I was forced to leave. Nowadays, especially for those who were not involved, this fact may seem insignificant; but in those days it counted for a great deal. To a limited extent I learnt what dictatorship meant and what an authoritarian system of government is capable of. I got into difficulties at school, and with the police, and finally had to accept what was to me an incomprehensible rejection at the hands of the infantry even though I had passed my officer's exam with merit. This blow put paid to my desire to become an active soldier, and early in 1937 I took my school leaving certificate in Lübeck, with the intention of going on to university. Before that, however, I had to do my labour service and military service. I performed my labour service in Camp Sörup near the Danish border.

Despite gratifyingly early recognition as a potential leader I was disappointed with the camp and the infantry, and began to think of the cavalry as an alternative. My own love of riding, my belief that the cavalry had no time for the politics of the day and finally, the knowledge that ancestors of my mother's had served with the Thirteenth Regiment of the King's Lancers in Hanover, were all factors which led me to volunteer for the Thirteenth Cavalry Regiment Lüneburg.

Joining the First Squadron of the Thirteenth Cavalry Regiment in Lüneburg at the beginning of November 1937 opened up a new and totally different world for me, especially after my bitter disappointment with the Hitler Youth, labour service, Party and State. At that time the men serving with the cavalry in Lübeck were almost without exception volunteers who came from farms and estates in Lower Saxony and Schleswig-Holstein. Right from the start I experienced in this circle the genuine friendship and freely given comradeship which I had hoped to find years before when I joined the Hitler Youth. Here it was taken for granted that at all times each of us was ready to do his best for the others.

But there was another essential factor which contributed to this life – our horses. We loved them; we cursed them; they were almost a part of ourselves and certainly a part of our community.

Neither during training nor after it was there any attempt at political schooling or party-political indoctrination in the cavalry ranks. We cavalry men led our own idiosyncratic lives. While military scientists were brewing up their evil plans for the first atom bomb, we were trotting, cantering and galloping with sabres raised towards straw-filled sacks stuck on poles. The object of this exercise was not so much to run through the enemy sack with our curved sabres but to keep the horses heading in the direction of these frightening straw monstrosities by applying constant, firm pressure with the insides of our thighs. I could never quite understand why my Nelly – a Hungarian mare and my four-legged companion for almost four years – was always terrified by these straw shapes, despite her general shrewdness and reliable instinct. Occasionally she even threw me several horse-lengths before the intended sabre encounter could take place.

The year 1939 came. In spite of the general feeling of restlessness and the latent uncertainty which characterized the immediate pre-war period, my parents and I made all the necessary preparations for me to begin my studies that autumn in Berlin, immediately my two years of military service were over. The enrolment formalities had been completed and lodgings found for me in Berlin when, at the end of July, I had a very bad fall from my horse and was forced to spend several months in the garrison hospital at Lübeck with a shattered tibia. I found it almost unbearable to be confined to hospital after war broke out on 1 September 1939. Since most of the regiment had no interest whatsoever in politics, we were completely taken aback by this turn of events.

Without delay my squadron was sent to the Western Front as part of the 158th Reconnaissance Unit of the Fifty-Eighth Infantry Division, formed in Lübeck. It had its baptism by fire in the Saarland near Perl, at the point where the German, French and Luxembourg borders converge.

The days of September 1939, the first month of the war, dragged on and on. Whenever news of military successes in Poland were broadcast over the radio I grew more terrified than ever that the war was going to be won without me. On receiving post from my squadron with news of their first battles and also of their first losses, I couldn't bear it any longer. I wrote petitions, made myself a nuisance to the doctors and was generally so troublesome that eventually I succeeded in obtaining permission to start walking again in early October, although this was almost certainly premature. I suffered a lot of pain before being allowed to rejoin my squadron. I was still hobbling with the aid of a stick and my leg was in plaster, when I got to the village called Igel near the Luxembourg border, where the squadron was stationed. It was early November.

During the first few weeks after leaving hospital and returning to my squadron I found riding and walking very painful. A final X-ray examination in December revealed that though the break had healed the broken bones had grown together crookedly. I didn't give a damn. All that mattered was that I was back in action, where from now on nothing could happen without me.

We spent the next few months training for the planned attack on France. During this period I was promoted to ensign-sergeant-major and spent my first wartime Christmas with the regiment. In January 1940 I was transferred for further training to the Cavalry Academy at Krampnitz near Berlin. We were put through hard physical and mental tests and we learnt how a young officer earns the respect of his soldiers. The ability to lead men is not a skill that can be learnt. You either have the gift or not. But even so it is vital to have models to look up to and experienced mentors to follow. The unit commander, Lieutenant-Colonel von Lengerke, who was later killed at Stalingrad, used to say whenever the fuss and pretentiousness of the young lieutenants and ensigns became too much for him, 'A gentleman is only conspicuous for his modesty and inconspicuousness.'

In spite of the stress of classes and examinations and my occasional visits to theatres, museums and concert halls in Berlin, my thoughts were always with my squadron and with my loyal horse. When the course came to an end and the results were announced, I was one of the few who had not passed and who had therefore failed to gain a commission as First Lieutenant. The final assessment of me, read out and commented upon by my instructing officer, Lieutenant Jürgens, a man I couldn't stand, went as follows: 'The Ensign-Sergeant-Major Gerhard Boldt has a forward and overbearing manner. He will first have to prove himself in action at the front.' It would be dishonest of me not to admit that at the time I was extremely annoyed and disappointed at this result. But even this apparent reversal had its good sides.

On 10 May 1940 German forces began the offensive against France, in which the Sixteenth Army, including my 158th Reconnaissance Unit, was involved. As a result of my failure at Krampnitz Academy I was sent straight back to my squadron after a short spell with the reserve section in Lüneburg, unlike my more successful companions who had been promoted to the rank of First Lieutenant. So it was that I was plunged into action during the first days of the advance.

The Sixteenth Army's route lay through Luxembourg,

through the foothills of the southern Belgian Ardennes and on towards the Maginot Line near Charleville – Mezières – Sedan – Carignan – Montmédy. I reached my squadron in south Belgium on 14 May, the fourth day of the campaign, shortly before it crossed the border into France. I felt then as if I had at last come home after a long journey, so great was my joy at being re-united with my friends and with my horse.

May 1940 was a warm, dry month. The main roads had been resurfaced by the motorized units advancing westwards. We rode along narrow minor roads and sandy lanes. The advance was very quickly over in this section of the front, and the German army communiqué of 18 May 1940 reported that St Quentin and Rethel had been taken; the communiqué of 21 May reported the fall of Arras, Amiens and Abbeville.

On the advance of the Sixteenth Army in the Sedan area the communiqué also reported that 'the German troops have gained some ground south of Sedan'. At this point the Sixteenth Army's advance was supposed to come to a halt. The flank of the German Army which had penetrated thus far westwards had to be protected. Histories of the Second World War record that battles on the approaches to the Maginot Line took place from 15 May to 6 June 1940. We dug ourselves in in the great bend of the Meuse between Mouzon and Stenay, on the hills of the north bank. Opposite us the French Front was several hundred yards away and only spasmodic mortar- and artillery-fire – partly from the heavy calibre guns of the outer defences of the Maginot Line near Montmédy – reminded us that it wasn't just a manoeuvre we were taking part in. Even nocturnal scouting parties in the no-man's-land between the fronts were by no means calculated to bring home to me the true nature of war.

At the beginning of June, however, this idyllic war came

to an abrupt end. On 5 June the German armies between Montmédy and the canal coast near Abbeville launched a major new thrust southwards. The Fifty-Eighth Division's task was to attack the enemy forces who were defending themselves in the extensive forests about fifteen miles southeast of Sedan. The enemy troops consisted largely of a North African colonial unit supported by heavy French artillery. They fought a superb battle of defence on the northern edge of the forest, and the two regiments of our Fifty-Eighth Infantry Division, which were in the front line of the attack, suffered heavy casualties. The Germans had not reckoned with such determined French resistance at this stage; their attack ground to a halt and the two regiments which had led the attack had to be withdrawn from the front. My reconnaissance unit was among the relief troops sent in to relieve them.

Up to that time nothing in my life had struck me with such direct force, so consciously, indeed brutally, as the experiences of those days near the forest. Our platoon's horses, bicycles and motor vehicles had been left behind with the baggage train several miles away from the front, so I had my first taste of war as a foot soldier. Our ears were constantly assailed by cries of despair and entreaty from the wounded in no-man's-land. At night we would go out searching for the dead and wounded between the fronts, breathing in the sickly-sweet pall of death which lay over the battlefield. During those weeks, in the face of death and the presence of my comrades' fear I overcame my own deepest fears. I still don't know why but again and again I forced myself, voluntarily, to make my way through the inferno of the French barrage from the fortifications of the Maginot Line in order to look for my comrades, sometimes as a messenger and sometimes simply to offer whatever help was needed. This triumph over myself proved a source of support and strength to me throughout the war.

In the wake of the victorious advance of the German divisions and armies along the entire front, the French abandoned the forest twenty-five kilometres south of Sedan, between 11 and 12 June. We immediately joined in the thrust towards Verdun, and at last got the opportunity to ride.

After a short fight on 14 June, Verdun fell with all its outer fortifications to the troops of the Sixteenth Army on 15 June, and we rode on in a south-easterly direction towards Toul. My reconnaissance unit and consequently also the First Squadron received orders from the division to make a detour round Toul and attack from the east. Departure time was fixed for our mounted squadron for two o'clock in the morning of 18 June and, in the meantime, we had a welcome break in a deserted village on the Toul road. It was a mild night, only a few days before the summer solstice, and we could already see the dawn rising as we sat on horseback awaiting our marching orders with some uneasiness. Our musings were suddenly interrupted by the sergeant's order to stand by to receive some champagne from the field kitchen, but there was no time to drink it before setting off. So we bound the fat-bellied bottles in an upright position behind the criss-crossed straps on our saddle-bags. I remember that ride into the dawn as if it were yesterday. First at walking-pace, then at a trot, we rode on towards Toul, the target of our attack, unobserved by the French. We turned into a broad avenue, bordered by old trees. A messenger from the scouting party ahead returned at a gallop and agitatedly reported roadblocks ahead. I galloped forward with the messenger, to take stock of the situation for myself. About two to three hundred metres farther on, just round the bend, the French had felled the old avenue-trees and made the road impassable for motor vehicles. Suddenly a shot rang out, then another. The leading column cantered up briskly, followed by the rest of the squadron: the signal to gallop was given, and we headed for the town with our sabres raised at full tilt, jumping over the felled trees. Everything worked like clockwork, just as we had practised it at home in Lüneburg. Nobody took any notice of the spasmodic firing. Then, suddenly, in the midst of this impressive mounted charge, loud, repeated detonations burst from the earth between our horses' hooves, as they galloped to clear the obstacles in their path. We were thrown into a state of near chaos as we rode into the attack. None of us had given a thought to the champagne bottles bound to our saddlebags, which were now detaching themselves as the result of our galloping and exploding on the ground.

As we reached the first buildings, the French rifle-fire increased. At first it was nothing more than an ineffective defensive volley on the part of a few sleepy Frenchmen, who were caught unawares and were, in the main, only half dressed. They had not expected a cavalry attack with drawn sabres accompanied by exploding champagne bottles. However they finally fell into line, and their defensive fire grew stronger. We dismounted and continued the attack on foot with rifles and machine guns. In the course of our continued infantry charge, I stormed a bridge over the Moselle with my men and forced an entry into the town. The enemy were now defending themselves with growing tenacity and bravery. During the street fighting I received a shot in the left side of my chest, just above the heart. That was the end of the French campaign for me. For this attack, however, I was later decorated with the Iron Cross, Class II, and the decoration for a wound sustained in action.

After a stay of several weeks in military hospital and a

subsequent period of convalescence I returned to my squadron in early autumn. It was then stationed in Flanders, busily engaged in preparing for the attack on Britain. Our reconnaissance unit was occupying the villages of Neerpelt and Overpelt near the Dutch border, and we spent the last months of 1940 there. Our relations with the local population were as pleasant as could be expected under the circumstances. During this period, to my great distress, I was transferred from my cavalry squadron to the motorized 'heavy weight' squadron, but in the course of my transfer I was promoted to the rank of First Lieutenant and as time went on and my responsibility grew, my assignment, which ranged from training to questions of equipment and motorization, gave me a lot of pleasure, despite my initial misgivings.

In April 1941, our lives suffered a great upheaval. The Fifty-Eighth Division, including my unit, was transferred by rail to East Prussia. We were filled with such regrets at leaving Flanders and its material comforts that it never occurred to us to wonder about the reason for our transfer. It certainly never entered my head for a moment that our move might have anything to do with a war against Russia.

My unit was stationed south of Elbing for the next two months. I delighted in and consciously made the most of this spring in East Prussia, with its lakes and forests, its landscape full of an enchanting melancholy and so many kind people for whom hospitality is the very essence of life.

Then we began to proceed farther and farther eastwards from Elbing, quickening our pace after 15 June, once summer had spread itself over the country. Near Heidekrug, only a short way from the German-Russian border, we were quartered and settled down to wait.

21 June 1941 came. In the late hours of the afternoon the

reconnaissance unit lined up in open square formation, facing east. Major Zietlow, a commander of great understanding and forbearance (especially as far as I and my extravagances were concerned), stepped out in front of our ranks with a clouded face and read out to us Adolf Hitler's orders to the soldiers of the Eastern Army to open hostilities against the Soviet Union. The attack was to begin that night. Hitler's orders concluded with the sentence, 'May the Lord God help us all in this battle.'

Our advance took us through Lithuania and Latvia: at Riga we crossed the Daugava and after about three weeks we were already marching through the burning town of Pleskau at the southern tip of Lake Peipus. During the first few weeks of our march through the Baltic countries my corps of engineers put its training to good use. The only two things against which even we cavalry engineers had no remedy were the heat and the dust. Two new experiences, in marked contrast, made our advance additionally memorable. First there was the excitement and the joy at deliverance with which the people in the Baltic provinces welcomed us. Secondly, there was the first evidence of the merciless cruelty which was to be a recurrent feature of this war in the east.

Our unit suffered its first losses only a few days after the invasion of Lithuania. Among them was the unit's doctor, who had been caught in an ambush set by some scattered Russian soldiers, and hideously mutilated. Admittedly, on the German side there was the infamous order which stated that commissars who had been taken prisoner were to be shot on the spot. In fact this order was not carried out by the majority of German companies, including our own division.

About six miles north of Pleskau both division and reconnaissance unit halted. We pitched camp under an open

20

sky, placing outposts to deal with any skirmishes. It was now that the war in the east began for us in earnest.

On 16 July we took the stubbornly defended little town of Gdow by storm. On 18 July I received orders to blow up a heavy military bridge over the River Narva, which was central to the enemy's eastern escape route, linking Lake Peipus to the Baltic. After this episode I returned on 19 July to my unit, to find them preparing for an attack on the ground defences on both sides of our advance route, part of the Stalin Line. During this attack I was wounded fairly severely and before I could even be carried off to the main dressing station I received the Iron Cross, Class I, the first member of the Fifty-Eighth Division to be so decorated in the Eastern Campaign.

I was forced to spend about two months in the infirmary in Stendal and then, after a short spell of sick leave, I returned to my squadron. We formed part of the Leningrad blockade, encamped at first on the Pulkovo Heights, and then near Uritsk, a suburb of Leningrad, and along the coastal road of the Gulf of Finland. The staff officers of our unit had made camp at Stelna, a little town between Peterhof and Leningrad, together with my corps of engineers who were standing by in reserve. During the night of 7 October the Russians launched an attack with heavy infantry and armoured divisions westwards from Leningrad, and it was now that my dedicated little band proved its worth. This battle lasted almost three days, its final outcome in doubt for most of that time. We played cat and mouse around the houses with Russian tanks, and at moments of total frustration in the battle I sought refuge at the piano I had unearthed in a school-room, playing melodies I had once played with my mother. I was deeply conscious once again of the unique satisfaction of overcoming personal fear.

Only one person out of my entire corps was wounded during the battle – myself. During the encounter with the tanks shell splinters hit me in the chest and in the upper thigh of my right leg. Nevertheless, as I could walk and bear the pain, I remained with my detachment. As a result of my wounds I was declared unfit for service and released for special assignments. I was also informed that I was to be awarded the Knight's Cross. I packed my car full of tobacco and cigarettes and drove to Estonia, where I bartered tobacco and petrol for butter, salmon, vodka and salmon-caviar, a punishable offence, but one which seemed worth the risk.

After my return to the front at Leningrad I found a news-reel camera team, war reporters and industrial experts on the scene. It seemed that our successful confrontation of tanks by manpower had caused a minor sensation. A photograph of me appeared on the front page of *Die Wehrmacht*, our forces' magazine; it was captioned 'the little king of Leningrad'. I must confess that this nickname had not originated solely in my activity in the front line. However my gratification at this new-found fame was spoiled by the news that it was not I but the commanding officer of our whole section, Colonel Kreipe, who was to receive the Knight's Cross.

By now the Russian winter had set in. The German Front on the Gulf of Finland near Uritsk and on the Pulkovo Heights was paralyzed. I had still not fully recovered from my most recent wounds and I gladly complied with the order from the German Armed Forces High Command to take some time off for studying. I went home, and, as far as I was concerned, the war ceased to exist for four months. I took up my studies in the Faculty of Foreign Affairs at the University of Berlin, as I was planning to try for a post in the

Foreign Office after the war. Apart from a certain amount of friction with the Nazi student society because I did not participate in its activities, and some unpleasant differences of opinion with members of the SS, this interruption of the war was for me a very lucky break.

In February and March 1942 more letters began to arrive from my friends on the Leningrad Front than had been the case in the previous months; they were in a critical situation as a result of vigorous and successful Russian thrusts. For the time being my division had been transferred, along with the infantry regiments, to the area north of Lake Ilmen; the reconnaissance unit was to follow. Nobody said anything more definite but I could read between the lines that the officers themselves and also the men of my engineering corps expected me to return to the unit as quickly as possible. I completed the semester and, without taking the leave owing to me, drove back to the front at the end of March 1942.

North of Lake Ilmen between Novgorod and Tshudovo, where the front line was formed by the River Volchov, there is – apart from a railway line and one single proper road – nothing but swamp, virgin forests, marshy water holes and desolate wastes. The reconnaissance unit was transferred to this wilderness. The fighting we had to endure in the following months was very hard indeed; but far worse was our struggle against the climate. In April, when the thaw set in, it seemed as if all the snow in Russia had melted into this spot on the Volchov. Our tents, combat platforms and communication lines had to be shifted onto rafts. For weeks the water in the marshy forests was more than three feet deep and our trenches were similarly affected. When the sun began to grow warm and the frost slowly but finally released its grip on the earth so that the water could seep through, we were assaulted by a rapidly multiplying plague of mosquitoes. Then there were the lice – an average day's bag consisted of eighty of them. Nor was I spared by Volchov fever, sometimes known as five-day fever. For years it has continued to remind me of this accursed place. To add to our distress the dressing-station was set up eleven miles away. In all, this was by far the worst experience I had to undergo during the entire war.

The battle to the north of Lake Ilmen against the encircled Second Russian Army's strike force under General Vlassov ended in early June. A mere thirty thousand Russian soldiers were taken prisoner out of the sixteen Russian divisions and brigades which had been surrounded. Tens of thousands had died of starvation in the swamps, or had drowned or perished miserably from their wounds. The sun beat down remorselessly on this horrifying field of corpses and swarms of insects hovered above in great clouds.

In June our division was withdrawn from the Volchov Front to recuperate – we too had suffered very heavy losses – and we returned to consolidate the line of defence in the Leningrad area, at the Oranienbaum pocket. I was appointed leader of a company of Russian volunteers, an assignment which, mercifully, only lasted two months; I cannot claim that I felt particularly happy and secure with this bunch of quixotic and shady characters. Life was so much brightened by the comforts, entertainment and general welfare of our new situation that it was easy to forget we were still in the front line, but by the beginning of December all this was over. At the end of November, to the south of Lake Ilmen, the Russians had launched their major offensive under the command of Marshal Timoshenko with four armies, the Eleventh, Thirty-Fourth, Fifty-Third, and the First Army of stormtroops. The operation was directed at the corridor roughly fifty kilometres long near Demyansk, defended by our northern armies.

From the very first day in our new positions along the southern front of the corridor, we were involved in constant defensive fighting. After Christmas we were withdrawn from the south front of the corridor and transferred to its northern edge, where the Russians had succeeded in making a small breach in our positions. In a counter-attack on 1 January 1943 I was slightly wounded but able to remain with my squadron. Then, in a renewed counter-attack, I was seriously wounded by splinters of tank shell and had to be carried off to the main dressing-station as soon as darkness fell. No hope was held out for the successful treatment of my wounds; but I was lucky enough to have friends who had connections with men at the top; they arranged for me to be flown out from the dressing-station and then taken by train in a first-class sleeping car from East Prussia to the Hindenburg military hospital in Berlin-Zehlendorf.

Thanks to the skill of the famous surgeon Weinke, and to the fact that I was in a well-equipped military hospital in Germany, my right leg was saved. It was many weeks before I recovered fully from the operation on my thigh, but my stay in hospital was not without its compensations. On my birthday, 24 January, I met Renate Sommerfeld, a nurse who was doing her auxiliary war training at the Hindenburg hospital. By March I was able to walk again, and soon afterwards we became engaged. We were married just before I was due to return to the service.

At the beginning of May 1943 I was awarded the Knight's Cross for my part in the defence of the Demyansk corridor. Our fortnight's honeymoon on the Wörther See in June came to a premature end when I received a telegram informing me that I had been allotted a new posting. However, my wife's influence had already made itself felt upon my military activities, for I had become a regular, largely as a result of the encouragement which she and her Prussian military family gave me. Four months later I was promoted to Cavalry Captain. When the telegram came I was not yet well enough to return to my unit so I spent the remaining six months of 1943 in France as the commander of the Heavy Squadron of the Bicycle Reconnaissance Unit, 389th Infantry Division, which was being drawn up around Saint-Lo in Normandy.

At the beginning of April 1944 I was instructed to proceed to the First Cavalry Division of the Royal Hungarian Army, where I was to head the German liaison staff. When I arrived in Kalusz, near Stryj in Galicia, at the beginning of April, I learnt that my staff, together with its cars, its interpreters and everything else required, was still at St Pölten in Austria being set up, and that it would probably only arrive at liaison staff headquarters on 4 or 5 May; moreover the First Cavalry Division to which my staff and I were attached did not even exist as a unit; it was still being set up in Eastern Hungary. The Chief of the Sixth Liaison Staff did not really know what to do with me, and so we both had the marvellous idea of sending me to Hungary to observe on the spot the setting up of the Royal Hungarian First Cavalry Division.

This turned out to be a tremendous stroke of luck. The flight from Stryj to Budapest was the beginning of a period which, even in retrospect, and even though it lasted only two months, seems like a marvellous dream. I left Galicia which was grey, dirty and mud-covered. The Carpathian Mountains, over which we had to fly, were still blanketed with snow. But when we landed in Budapest, we found ourselves in glorious springtime, which made this jewel among the cities of Europe seem infinitely more attractive. I had to spend several days there for consultations with the Military Attaché and I stayed as an honoured guest in the world-famous Gelert Hotel, 'supported' by my Knight's Cross. After all the filth and the distress which I had seen in the past few years these days in Budapest, which seemed almost untouched by the war, had something strange and unreal about them.

I went over my instructions for setting up the First Cavalry Division with the Military Attaché, and then I left Budapest for Nyiregyháza in Eastern Hungary, where my duties as a liaison officer really began. The day after my arrival I reported to the Commanding Officer of what was to become the First Cavalry Division, H. E. Lieutenant-General von Vàtaxy the former ADC to von Horthy, the Hungarian Regent, and immediately received a private invitation from him to come to his home. Here I was received with utterly charming courtesy and hospitality, such as is completely unknown in Germany. At this small reception in my honour I was also given my first official commission. Whether it was because His Excellency wanted in this way to get to know me, or because he wanted to show me something of his beautiful country, or simply to give me a particular treat – whatever the reason, this commission must have been one of the most unusual and pleasant ones which were ever allotted in the history of the German Army.

His Excellency ordered that I was to go out riding early every morning with his daughter, who was about twenty years old and a brilliant and enthusiastic horsewoman. So, every morning, out we went into the countryside on fine, fast thoroughbreds, sometimes breakfasting with friends on neighbouring estates. My excursions also brought me a large

27

number of invitations through which I got to know both the country and its people, and learned to love and respect them. I made friends then who stood by me during the worst battles of the Russian campaign. Indeed, they even saved my life.

Of all the invitations I received the one which remains most firmly fixed in my memory was that of Count Cároly, a cousin of the then Prime Minister. My two-day visit was like a journey to a different world – from my reception by the Count's family on the broad stairs in front of the château, my private viewing of his collection of copperplate engravings, the drive in the family's coach and four through the village with its school and church, to the most exquisite delicacies from the Count's kitchen and cellar. The Countess showed me to my room, her own room in fact, where, she told me, she had given birth to her two children. On the piano a bouquet of thirty crimson roses had been placed to welcome me. The view from the room and its wide balcony was one of an extensive park, with peacocks, pheasants, black swans and white swans, and an enclosure in which some fine horses were trotting about.

When the division left Hungary about two weeks later and was transferred to Russia, one of the Count's servants brought me a letter from the Countess containing a pressed crimson rose. Both the Count and the Countess hoped that I would return home safe and unharmed from this terrible war. The pressed rose was one of the thirty which had stood on the piano in my room at Naydmagosch to welcome me; it was now to serve me as a talisman and a keepsake. And, somehow, it did.

The evening before the divisional staff left Hungary, some of us were invited by His Excellency to Shoshdo, an inn just outside Nyiregyháza, to take our leave of Hungary. Gypsies played while we ate and drank and we danced to their music: the General's daughter and my friends taught me how to dance a Zcardash. But it was no use, the imminent parting overshadowed everything. I spent a long time that evening sitting with my friend Count Stipsy, a Captain of the Reserve with estates in south Hungary. He sung a sad Hungarian song and we talked about life, marriage and beautiful women.

About 15 June 1944 I arrived in the assembly area, in the Pripiet marshes, about eighty kilometres south-east of Baranovitski, with the last units of the division. Here the division was placed under the Second Army, as part of Army Group Central. On 22 June the Russians began their massive summer offensive against the Army Group Central, and in the course of this attack the German Fourth and Ninth Armies were almost completely destroyed. On 3 July the division was thrown into defensive action with the Fourth Cavalry Brigade, on the northern edge of the Pripiet marshes. Right from the start the casualties of the division and its losses of equipment were very high, and the fighting very fierce. I did everything I possibly could to help my Hungarian friends in the first weeks of what was for them the new experience of war. At last, towards the end of July, the German Front consolidated and it became possible for the division to be withdrawn from the front for rest and re-equipment.

After three weeks I was recalled by telegram to Hirschberg in Silesia to take a General Staff course. Field-Marshal Model at Army Group Centre headquarters was loath to let me go: 'What do you mean, they want you to join the General Staff? I can't do without you here: you are staying in Hungary. The war's lost anyway,' he told me. Then, after a short pause he added, 'You'll get along much better after the war as a Captain than as a General Staff Officer.' So I didn't go.

The division's rest period lasted about a fortnight; we left Niewikla on 20 August and on 25 August the division took over responsibility for part of the front, east of Warsaw, the last German bridgehead to the east of the Vistula. At the end of August the Hungarian government fell, following hard upon Roumania's revocation of her alliance with Germany and her subsequent declaration of war on us. The southern front was moved up to the frontier between Hungary and Roumania. The Hungarians planned to bring all their troops still in Russia back to Hungary to defend their country. The Royal Hungarian First Cavalry Division duly began the withdrawal of its units, and on 27 September the division began the move back to Hungary by rail. On 9 October I reported back to divisional battle H.Q. in Kecskemet, a strategically important town for the safety of Budapest. Next day the Russians launched an armoured attack on Kecskemet, and the town was temporarily lost, with heavy casualties on both sides. But we reoccupied the town on the same day, and when I returned to my quarters to rest, I received a visit from my friend Stipsy. I hardly recognized him: he had always been the soul of cheerfulness and energy, but now he seemed exhausted and full of despair. He brought me news, *inter alia*, of the Cároly family, with whom he had been on friendly terms. They, the Count, the Countess and their two children, had all committed suicide when Russian troops invaded their estate.

Now that the war was being waged on Hungarian soil and reports of Russian atrocities committed on the civilian population were increasing daily, and as the defence of Hungary began to look more and more hopeless, on 12 and 13 October I was visited at liaison staff H.Q. by several Hungarian friends of mine, junior officers of the Second and Fourth 'Hadik' Hussar Regiments. They came without the knowledge

30

of divisional headquarters. These junior officers told me that according to rumours from reliable sources close to the government in Budapest another change of government was to be expected in the next few days, and that this would probably be followed by the Hungarians' defection from the German-Hungarian alliance, as had happened in Roumania. Large numbers of troops, including whole units, had already gone over to the enemy from the division immediately next to ours, the Twenty-Third Hungarian Infantry Division.

Between us we decided on a plan of action by which they agreed to try and discover from their own contacts what was going on in the Budapest government circles and to sound out and confirm the support of those elements in the Hungarian forces willing to continue fighting on the German side. For my part I promised to prepare a plan to disengage the German troops as well as the pro-German Hungarian troops in the battle area between the Danube and the Theis. All this was to be carried out in the strictest secrecy, as the attitude of divisional H.Q. on this situation was still ambiguous.

I made contact with Count von Nostiz, Chief of Staff of the Army Corps to which the First Hungarian Cavalry Division belonged. I gave him a rough outline of the political situation and asked for an interview with the commanding officer, General Kirchner, as soon as possible. Von Nostiz promised his support. On 14 October, sixteen officers of the division met at my quarters. Reports from Budapest said that Hungary was intending to break with Germany on the following Saturday at 2.0 pm, and that a very large part of the Hungarian Army was expected to surrender simultaneously. As large sections of the front were being held by Hungarian troops alone, this meant, effectively, the collapse of the entire Hungarian Front and the danger of the German troops still fighting in Hungary being taken prisoner. The plan which

I had worked out provided that both the German troops fighting between the Danube and the Theis and those Hungarian troops who wanted to continue fighting on the German side should withdraw to the Danube crossing at Dünaföldvár and form a bridgehead there; otherwise, the west bank of the Danube was to be defended. This plan was approved without reservation by the Hungarian officers who were present.

That evening I finally heard from Count von Nostiz that he had arranged an appointment with General Kirchner for the next day. General Kirchner was furious. I had briefed both Kirchner and Nostiz thoroughly about the explosive political situation and the measures which I had already taken. But Kirchner was afraid of complications with the Hungarian government as a result of my unauthorized actions; he thought the whole thing was stupid gossip, which would get him into trouble with his political and military superiors in Germany; and he told me abruptly to stop all my activities in this direction. I was extremely angry, and drove back to my liaison staff headquarters, damning the General; from then on I intensified my activities along the same lines as before. In the evening I called my liaison staff together. I explained the situation and announced the emergency plan due to take effect on Saturday at 2.0 pm, so that every single man knew what he had to do. As we had to expect the possibility of attack by anti-German Hungarian troops and Russians who would seize the opportunity to break through our lines, a full supply of ammunition was issued.

I hardly slept that night: messengers were coming all the time, bringing news from Budapest, and from the units of the strengthened Hungarian Cavalry Division about the situation there. According to these reports a Hungarian defection at 2.0 pm the following day seemed inevitable, and the situation in the Army was completely confused, so that we must be prepared for anything.

At 1.30 pm on Saturday the telephone rang. It was the divisional commander, Lieutenant-Field-Marshal von Ibraniy, in person, asking me to come over immediately to his headquarters, only about a hundred yards from the German liaison staff headquarters; he wanted, he said, to speak to me. I gave my staff hurried orders that if I had not reported back by 2.10 pm they were to attack the divisional headquarters, free me if possible and then fight their way through towards Dünaföldvár immediately.

Once again we synchronized watches, and then I hurried off, uncertain of what awaited me. Ibraniy himself received me at the Hungarian headquarters most hospitably. We sat down with the officers of the staff, had a drink, toasted one another and made small talk. The hands of the clock moved on remorselessly, Ibraniy smiling every time I looked at my watch, as though amused. It was probably about four or five minutes to two when Ibraniy stood up and said, smiling almost affectionately, 'My dear Captain, you ought to have let me in on your conspiracy, because I am with you as well. And now please hurry up and ring up your staff before they attack us!' Later that day the news arrived that on the Carpathian Front the First Hungarian Army had gone over to the enemy almost *en bloc* – at 2.0 pm.

On 17 October the division, containing the crack troops of the Hungarian Army, was renamed the Royal Hungarian First Hussar Division. I managed, with the help of my connections, to get Colonel Schell transferred: he became the Commanding Officer of the Hungarian First Tank Division.

On 20 October a certain Major Huck arrived at liaison staff headquarters with instructions, to my amazement, to take over from me, but the news soon reached me that I had been transferred to the Führer's staff at Army High Command.

The battle area moved gradually farther south. My unit left Kecskemet, and I went back to the front on my own to look for my Hungarian friends and to say goodbye to them. Near Kiskunhálas I came upon a troop of Hungarian cavalry who had made an unsuccessful offensive and who were now debating what to do. Among them was my friend Count Stipsy, whose estates were nearby: he was standing somewhat apart from the rest, with about twenty volunteer troopers gathered around him. The Hungarians were undecided. Then Stipsy straightened up in his saddle, called out something to his soldiers, turned round to me, standing straight as a die in his stirrups, and called out, with his most dazzling smile, '*Bartchi*, have a safe journey home. Goodbye – and don't forget me!' Then off they galloped, all twenty of them, bent forward over their horses, their captain at their head. One of them returned the following night: all the rest had been killed by Russian machine-gun fire.

On 26 October 1944 I left Hungary, and have never returned.

1. BRIEFING IN THE REICH CHANCELLERY

Berlin: early February 1945. The Wilhelmplatz stood cold and deserted, a mere cluster of burnt-out houses. Crumbling walls with gaping windows reared up amidst acres of rubble as far as the eye could see. Of the old Reich Chancellery, a neo-baroque palace which once proudly symbolized the Kaiser Wilhelm era, now only the ruined façade remained. The one building which stood apparently intact was the new Reich Chancellery, with its small rectangular balcony from which Adolf Hitler had received the tumultuous adulation of the German people. Huge and menacing, built in the bombastic style of National Socialist architecture, the broad façade of the Führer's Chancellery extended the whole length of the Vossstrasse, from the Wilhelmplatz to the Hermann-Göring-Strasse. Soldiers of Hitler's guard stood on duty outside, tall, strong lads, such as had long since disappeared from the streets of German towns.

Some weeks before, Hitler had retreated into the subterranean labyrinth of bunkers beneath and in the garden of the Chancellery, and now the heavy iron ramps which sealed off all entries to the bunkers during air-raids were already half-closed in readiness. Every day Hitler held a '*Führerlage*', a military briefing in the Chancellery. All three armed services took part in these conferences, at which recent military developments were discussed and decisions reached affecting the conduct of war by land, sea and air: that day I was to be taken to one of these conferences and introduced to Hitler for the first time.

The huge Mercedes of the Chief of the General Staff drew up in front of the gigantic square pillars of the new Chancellery on the right-hand side – the armed-forces entrance. The other entrance, on the left, was kept strictly separate for party members – a significant distinction. General Guderian, Chief of the German General Staff, stepped out, followed first by his adjutant, Major von Freytag-Loringhoven, and then myself. The sentries presented arms and we walked past them through the heavy oak doors into the Chancellery.

In the high entrance hall we were presented with a bleak prospect, made even drearier by the sparse light shed by the few remaining lamps. All the pictures, carpets and tapestries which had formerly hung there had long since been removed because of the increasingly frequent air-raids on Berlin. Huge cracks stretched across the ceiling and one of the walls; many of the window-panes had been replaced with cardboard or wood, and on the side facing the old Reich Chancellery, a wooden partition had been constructed to conceal the bomb-damage. An orderly asked for my official pass; I had neither this nor an equivalent warrant so my name had to be checked off in the long official list. Finally I was allowed to pass through. The Major took me a little way along to the Army Adjutancy (ADC's room) and there introduced me to Army Adjutant (ADC) Lieutenant-Colonel I. G. Borgmann, asking him at the same time whether the briefing was to be in Hitler's operations room or in the bunker: as there was no danger of an air-raid at the time, the briefing was arranged for Hitler's large operations room.

We continued through countless corridors and ante-rooms. At the head of each corridor our passes were inspected by further SS sentries. Our route was more roundabout than usual because of the heavy bomb-damage the Chancellery had suffered, particularly in the great ceremonial courtyard, which was completely destroyed. By contrast, the wing which housed Hitler's operations room was still largely undamaged: here the floor was still highly polished, the walls covered with paintings and the windows hung with sumptuous curtains. Immediately outside the ante-room in the conference area we were subjected to yet another, even more rigorous check by several SS officers and SS guards armed with machine-guns. We surrendered our weapons and our brief-cases were taken away and examined: since the attempted coup of 20 July 1944 brief-cases had been particularly suspect. We were not physically searched but the SS officers ran a well-trained eye over our tight-fitting uniforms. Inevitably our passes were scrutinized yet again, and then, at last, we were allowed to proceed to the ante-room.

We were too early; it was only 3.45 and the ante-room was still deserted except for three orderlies standing next to tables of refreshments and three more armed SS officers standing on the other side of the room outside the door leading to the conference room itself.

General Guderian took advantage of the delay to make a last-minute telephone call to Army High Command in Zossen to get the latest news of the eastern front. Eventually Hitler's personal adjutant, SS *Sturmbannführer* Günsche arrived and invited the Major and myself to go into the operations room as soon as Hitler had finished his consultation with Bormann. A few minutes later Bormann appeared at the door of the operations room. He looked about forty-five or fifty, average height, squat and stocky, bullnecked. His face was round with prominent cheek-bones and broad nostrils and wore an expression close to brutality. His eyes and the set of his features suggested cunning; his thinning hair was combed smoothly back. I gazed in fascination at the man who was said to exert such influence on Hitler, to be the evil genius behind the Führer's commands. After a brief greeting we followed Günsche past him into the operations room.

The room was long and very high, and contained very little furniture, though its floor was richly carpeted. Hitler's desk stood out prominently at the opposite end of the room, surrounded by a few small, upholstered chairs. One wall was broken up by four narrow, ceiling-high windows, hung with heavy grey curtains, and a glass door, through which we glimpsed the Chancellery garden. An elaborate marble map-table stood half-way along the wall, its black upholstered chair so placed that Hitler could look out on to the garden. On the map-table there was only a telephone, an electric bell, two unusually heavy paper-weights, a desk set and a few coloured pencils. The only other objects in the room were a heavy, round table, massive leather arm-chairs and a couch, arranged along the left and right walls.

The Major and I began to lay out the large General Staff maps in the prearranged order on the map-table – on top the maps of the Hungarian Front, at the bottom those of the Curland Front. Günsche stood behind watching us closely throughout. It took only a few minutes; and by four o'clock we were back in the ante-room, where most of the participants in the conference had now gathered. They were standing around or sitting in small groups, talking earnestly over their coffee or schnapps and sandwiches. General Guderian beckoned to me to join him, and introduced me to his companions, Field-Marshal Keitel, Chief of Army High Command, General Jodl, Chief of Army General Staff, Admiral of the Fleet Dönitz, and *Reichsleiter* Bormann. Looking around I saw their adjutants standing in a group nearby, and, over in the corner SS *Reichsführer* Himmler talking to General Fegelein, General of the *Waffen* SS, SS *Obergruppenführer* and Himmler's permanent representative to Hitler. Fegelein's arrogant manner resulted from the fact that his wife, Gretl Braun, was the sister of Eva Braun, whom Hitler was later to marry. He behaved as if he were already the Führer's brother-in-law. Kaltenbrunner, the much-feared head of the Reich Security Central Office, stood a little apart, engrossed in a document. Lorenz, permanent representative to Hitler of the Reich Press, stood talking to SS *Standartenführer* Wilhelm Zander, Bormann's permanent adviser. *Reichsmarschall* Göring sat with his staff officers Generals Koller and Christian at a round table in the middle of the room. Soon General Burgdorf, Hitler's chief adjutant, walked across the ante-room and into the operations room, reappearing in the doorway shortly afterwards. 'The Führer would like you to come in,' he said; we all lined up behind Göring, in order of rank, and followed him in.

Hitler was standing alone in the middle of the huge room, facing the doorway. We approached him in the same order and he greeted almost everyone individually with a silent handshake. Occasionally he asked a question of someone which was answered with a brief 'Yes, Führer' or 'No, Führer'. I stood near the door, nervously awaiting the approaching ordeal. General Guderian must have mentioned me to Hitler for I saw him glance at me and then Guderian signalled me to join them. I walked across to Hitler and the Führer shuffled slowly towards me, bowed and feeble. He stretched out his right hand and I felt a loose and flabby handshake, quite devoid of strength or feeling. His head shook slightly, a thing which was to strike me even more forcibly later. His left arm hung limply by his side and his left hand trembled perceptibly. All his movements were those of a sick, almost senile old man. His face, especially around the eyes, spoke of total weariness and exhaustion. Only in his eyes was there an indescribable, flickering brightness which had an alarming, totally unnatural effect, and the glance he gave me was strangely penetrating.

This was not the vigorous, energetic Hitler the Germans knew, the Hitler that Goebbels, Reich Minister for Propaganda, still depicted. He turned and shuffled slowly over to his table, accompanied by Bormann, and sat down facing the pile of maps we had laid there. The briefing was to begin with the so-called '*Westlage*', the military situation in the south-east, south-west, west and north. These combat zones were under the supervision of the Chief of Army High Command, but General Keitel did not appear to be interested. Indeed, he stood to one side and allowed General Jodl to take the floor. Among the younger officers Keitel was nicknamed 'Reich Garage Attendant', a label directed not so much at his character as at his strictly limited authority. There could not have been a more apt description of his true role, for the only independent operational or strategic powers he still held were over the petrol supplies of the Reich. In all other spheres of military command this field-marshal merely put his signature to Hitler's orders, for appearances' sake.

General Jodl began his report in a hushed, calm voice. The Führer could not bear loud voices in his presence and Jodl angled the presentation of his report to suit Hitler's wishes in every possible way.

'Führer, four tanks in Army Group E in the south-east were knocked out. In this area we were able to achieve our objectives. South of the Drau the disengagement of the units is making good progress. On both sides of the Sarajevo-Brod Strasse the 104th Rifle Division made some advances. In the Croatia-Serbia border zone, on the Drina, the 22nd Infantry Division has made further headway. Strong guerilla forces have infiltrated the Slovene area. The supreme commander in the south-east sets his own strength at 25,000 men. Against this the 22nd Infantry Division will be relieved by the intervention of sections of the 114th Rifle Division. The Cetniks are advancing in the direction of Tuzla, which ought to be an advantage to our units in the whole of this Serbian border area.'

There was a short pause to allow the maps to be changed. Hitler continued to sit in unbroken silence, merely lifting his arm a little so that the map of the south-eastern combat area could be removed. Jodl then went on with his report, this time dealing with Army Group C in the Italian battle area to the south-west.

'On the Italian Front, Führer, the enemy is intensifying his reconnaissance, otherwise there are only minor engagements to report. The withdrawal of the 356th Infantry Division to Hungary is going ahead according to plan. The Sixteenth SS *Panzergrenadier* Division is assembling in order to be ready for the withdrawal.'

At this point Jodl drew attention to the success of a small company of engineers in the area north of Florence. He was doing his utmost to please Hitler, who was obviously not in the best of tempers that day, lauding the prowess of these individual units in an attempt to distract him from the harsh overall picture. The truth of the matter was that both German armies had been driven back by fierce fighting to a line north of Florence. However, Hitler interrupted his digression with an impatient movement of his hand, and Jodl continued his report on the armies, moving on to the western Front. Hitler sat, as before, hunched over the table, staring fixedly through his glasses at the map. The upper half of his body was supported, as if powerless, on his forearms.

'Führer, in the west, on the lower Meuse, our bridgeheads have held out against fierce attacks by the First Canadian Army. The enemy bridgehead over the Oure, near Army Group B, has been boxed in. However, our reserves, the Twelfth *Volksgrenadier* Division, the Third *Panzargrenadier* Division and the Ninth SS Tank Division were tied down by fierce enemy attacks, which also encroached on the left flank of the Fifteenth Army.'

The situation in the west had clearly been very much affected by the Ardennes defeat. Troops on both sides were regrouping, and after this reversal signs of a possible German victory were, with the best will in the world, not to be found. So once again Jodl singled out an individual achievement, and began to sing the praises of a particular sergeant who had taken some prisoners in a shock-troop operation north of Hollerath. But Hitler impatiently interrupted Jodl in the middle of the story and signalled him to go on with his report on the situation in the west.

'Near Army Group C, in the area of the Nineteenth Army, the enemy thrust on Breisach continues. In the Colmar area some counter-attacks have been successful. The withdrawal of the Twenty-Fifth *Panzergrenadier* Division has been substantially completed. On the southern front of the army group there is only light combat activity.

'The supply position in the fortresses on the Atlantic coast may be regarded as satisfactory. La Rochelle has supplied the Gironde delta with personnel and supplies which has made possible an adequate reinforcement of the sea blockade of Bordeaux.

'The regrouping in Norway, following on the continued withdrawal of the 199th Infantry Division, is going according to plan. The bad weather in the northern Baltic area is interrupting the evacuation of troops from Oslo.

'From Denmark only minor sabotage operations are reported. The sixteen Marsch battalions which are due to be evacuated are assembling. The 20,000 men from the Baltic area who are to be handed over by the Commander-in-Chief of the Navy will undergo training as infantrymen in Denmark.'

Jodl had finished. Keitel had not uttered a single word throughout: it was left to Göring, who had now and then put in a word, to express his unauthoritative opinion on the conduct of the war on land, and in the discussion that followed Bormann also took some part.

Hitler seemed satisfied with Jodl's report. He raised himself up a little in his chair and turned to Keitel's adjutant, Lieutenant-Colonel von John. 'John, see to it that these two old gentlemen get into the bunker in good time during air-raids,' he said jokingly. Hitler's good opinion of these two colleagues was clearly based on the fact that they never failed to adapt themselves to his moods and never openly contradicted him. Their behaviour sanctioned his position as Commander-in-Chief, and that was precisely what he demanded from his close associates.

The next to speak was General Guderian, whose report covered the position in the east. He began with a survey of the overall position on the eastern Front.

'Army Group South in the area of Lake Balaron has repulsed enemy attacks on its southern front. The garrison

43

of Dunapentele, which was cut off, has been withdrawn. Here the intention is to shift the front further back and to incorporate the Velencze-See in the line of the front. Troop concentrations in the area south of Stuhlweissenburg and north of the bend in the Danube indicate a forthcoming attack by the Russians. The position of the encircled garrison in Budapest grows hourly worse. Supplies, ammunition and rations could be flown in and dropped but do not come anywhere near meeting the need. There is fighting around the castle. The Soviets have penetrated about one kilometre into the western front of the encircling ring.

'As regards Army Group Central, the Army Group Heinrici is involved in a disengagement from the "buffalo" position, which is in imminent danger of being penetrated in several places by the enemy. On our side counter-thrusts have been made. The enemy bridgehead at Ratibor has been strengthened. The army group here is replacing the Twentieth Tank Division. Some successes have been achieved against the enemy bridgeheads on both sides of Oppeln. On the other hand, the Soviets have been able to extend their bridgehead at Ohlau. In the bridgehead at Steinau the situation has again been aggravated. There is fighting in Steinau itself. Twenty-seven enemy tanks were knocked out near Kulm. General von Saucken's corps has fought its way through to the Oder and is preparing to cross it.

'In the area of Army Group Vistula, our units are disengaging east of Glogau. Strong attacks on all sides are reported from the enemy-encircled town of Posen. In the hospitals of Posen there are still more than two thousand wounded. The supply position is worse than critical. In the area north-east of Frankfurt on the Oder there is fighting near Bischofssee and Sonneburg. Near Küstrin the Soviet spearhead has been repulsed. Near Zielenzig, north-west of Küstrin, the Russians have succeeded in building a bridgehead on the west bank of the Oder. The Tirschtigel line has been penetrated in several places. Schwiebus and Schneidemühl have been surrounded. There is fighting near Kienitz, Neudamm and Freienwalde. The Thorn garrison, which is making a sortie in a north-easterly direction, has gained some more ground. There is fighting around Schloss Marienburg. Near Elbing contact towards the west has been re-established. In East Prussia Heilsberg and Friedland have been lost. Our own attack met with no success. There is fighting south-west of Königsberg. Here the Russians are blocking the Haff-Strasse. North of Königsberg the enemy has achieved further successes. Enemy attacks in Samland have been repulsed.

'Only minor fighting is reported from the Curland Front. The supply position here is satisfactory. The evacuation of the Third SS Corps and of the remainder of the Fourth Tank Division and of the Thirty-Second Infantry Division is going according to plan. Furthermore the 389th and the 281st Infantry Divisions are being withdrawn.'

The manner in which this report was delivered was terser and more to the point, and had none of the obliging style of Jodl's report. This was chiefly due to the vastly different character of this general; but his attitude to Hitler had also been very much affected by his experiences in 1941, when, after the failure of the German offensive on Moscow some very hard words had been exchanged and Hitler had sent Guderian 'home'. Hitler did not like the man; he found his independence of mind irritating, and had used him as a scapegoat for the failure of the Moscow campaign, his own brain-child. But after the attempted assassination of 20 July 1944 Hitler found himself rather badly off for generals. He had dismissed General Zeitzler, then Chief of the General Staff, and found that General Buhle, whom he wanted as a replacement, was too ill to serve. As a result Guderian, whose outstanding record as a tank commander must have been fresh in Hitler's memory, was appointed to the vacant post.

Guderian's return to active military service had not happened at a particularly auspicious time. Hitler's faith in the whole German officers' corps was badly shaken by the attempted coup, particularly his faith in the General Staff. He managed to maintain a reasonably civil relationship with Guderian for a few months after his appointment, but, in November 1944, there had once again been bitter clashes between them. Their mutual hostility was partly due to basic differences of opinion about military tactics; but a strong additional factor, and one which will always redound to Guderian's credit, was the way in which the General mustered the courage, time and again, openly to contradict and warn Hitler. He was one of the very few men in Hitler's entourage who stood by his own views and who were bold enough to contradict the Führer without restraint at that time.

After the failure of the Ardennes offensive, which had begun on 16 December 1944, Hitler had grown obsessed with the idea that he must not allow himself to be driven into the defensive. He firmly believed that it was possible to blind the enemy to his own weaknesses with offensive strategy. He, Adolf Hitler, must remain on the offensive at any price – that was the political and military axiom of his life. Naturally he also wanted to gain time. Guderian completely disagreed. He believed the German fronts were far too long; he thought

Germany's resources were nowhere near sufficient to remain both offensive, on the one hand, and then, on the other hand to maintain an adequately strong defensive line, particularly in the east. Guderian was only too well aware that the German lines of defence in the east were stretched to their utmost limits, and his chief objective, as he saw it, was to stop the Red Army getting into Central Europe. He therefore suggested the mobilization of all available military forces for the formation of a strong line of defence in the east. He knew that this could only have been achieved by weakening the western front, regardless of heavy reversals, and by forgoing all offensive successes in abandoning the Curland Front. Nevertheless Guderian was determined to make Hitler see reason. He drove from Zossen to Hitler's 'Eagle's Eyrie' headquarters near Bad Nauheim (Hitler had left the 'Wolf's Lair' headquarters in Eastern Prussia in order to take personal charge of the western offensive) on Christmas Eve 1944. At the risk of his own life the General demanded that Hitler break off the hopeless Ardennes offensive and immediately redirect the released units to the severely threatened eastern front. At this point Guderian forecast 12 June 1944 as the most likely date for the Russian attack.

Hitler declined to follow Guderian's advice. Instead he ordered 'Operation North Wind' for New Year's night 1944. He hoped that with this offensive he could win back Alsace, wipe out the American Seventh Army divisions stationed there, gain the prestige of a new victory and reopen the deadlocked Ardennes campaign on whose success he had pinned so much hope and staked his own reputation. These imagined military successes were the sort of wishful thinking in which Hitler frequently indulged and whose apogee was the total destruction of the Americans and the British. All this was in complete contradiction to the true position in the west, and in spite of urgent reports of an imminent large-scale attack by the Russians, from the Narev bridgehead and the three Vistula bridgeheads at Varka, Pulavy and Baranov.

Guderian did not give up easily. On 31 December 1944 he went once again to see Hitler at 'Eagle's Eyrie', and once again requested reserves and reinforcements for the eastern front. He tried to convince Hitler of the colossal danger building up in the east by showing him the detailed records of Russian strength and movements which had been compiled by General Gehlen's Military Intelligence department. These documents all pointed to 12 January as the most likely date for a Russian attack. Hitler was not convinced; but Guderian was not finished yet. On 9 January he tried yet again to bring the true situation home to Hitler, producing fresh documentary evidence. Again 12 January was given as the date fixed for a Russian attack. But even now Hitler would have none of it. He called General Gehlen's reports 'completely idiotic', 'a bare-faced bluff'. He could not believe in these Russian troop concentrations and preparations for attack because they didn't suit his plans. He made it quite clear that as far as he was concerned 'the eastern front must get by with what it has'. Needless to relate, the Russian attack began, at the Vistula and the Narev, south and north of Warsaw, on 12 January, just as had been predicted. Because of the weakness of our eastern front in the face of their huge forces almost the whole line of defence between East Prussia and the Carpathians collapsed after only two days. Occupied Poland was lost, and Silesia, most of Eastern Prussia and all the German provinces east of the Oder, except Outer Pomerania, followed. Now the Red Army stood at Küstrin, this side of the Oder, at the very gates of Berlin.

Guderian had finished his report, and, bowing slightly, he stepped back. There was a short discussion during which I removed the last map from the table and then General Christian of Air Force operations staff came forward to begin his report on the situation in the air. Göring and his Chief of Staff, General Koller, stood on one side, listening.

'Führer, thirty-eight missions were flown by our fighter pilots in support of our troops in the Monschau area. Ten "Mosquitoes" were shot down making for Berlin. About 900 British four-engined bombers made a daylight punitive raid on Ludwigshafen. The enemy attacked Vienna with 450 four-engined planes. A further 150 planes attacked Deutz. Further attacks by one- and two-engined planes were. . . .'

Meanwhile Guderian had approached Grand Admiral Dönitz and gone with him to the back of the room. Watching them, I was reminded of an incident which occurred between the Admiral and myself, putting me greatly in his debt. It had happened earlier in the month when I was not feeling too confident in my new position as ADC to the Chief of the General Staff and not yet capable of carrying out my duties in a completely routine way. On one occasion von Freytag-Loringhoven had stayed behind in Zossen and I had to accompany General Guderian alone to the briefing in the Reich Chancellery. It was to take place in the operations room, and before it began I was left alone in the room, under the surveillance of Hitler's personal SS adjutant, Günsche, to lay out the maps in order on Hitler's table, ready for Guderian's report. As a general rule he began with Hungary and ended with Curland. Unfortunately, instead of laying the Curland map down first so that he would get to it last, I carelessly laid the map of Hungary down first and that of Curland at the top. This may seem a slight enough offence to the outsider but in fact it was almost a capital crime.

General Burgdorf called the gentlemen in from the ante-room to the operations room to begin the discussion. Hitler greeted each of them and took his usual place in the chair in front of the map-table. Guderian stood on the left, ready to give his report, and I stood immediately to Hitler's right, ready to remove the maps in sequence as the report progressed. General Guderian began with the situation in Hungary. In the middle of the first sentence he stopped and glared at me. Hitler looked me up and down silently with an indescribable glance and leant back in his chair with a weary gesture. Realizing my error I began to stammer incoherently and the entire company stared at me as if I were a desperate criminal. Only Grand Admiral Dönitz smiled at me, said a few consoling words, lifted the pile of maps and requested me with a nod to lay them out again in the correct order. The incident was quickly forgotten and I conceived a lasting affection for the Admiral as a result of his kindness.

Dönitz's special influence on Hitler was not lost on Guderian. He knew that Dönitz had a better chance than he did of carrying a point with the Führer. The conversation between them concerned the Curland Front. Whatever happened Guderian wanted to bring back into the Reich the Sixteenth and Eighteenth Armies which were isolated on the Curland Front, along with the twenty-three divisions strengthening the eastern front in the Berlin sector. The breakthrough to East Prussia which Guderian had demanded of Hitler again and again during the closing months of 1944 was now out of the question. But it was not too late to plan an evacuation of the troops by sea from the two Curland ports of Wendau and Libau. Speed was of the utmost importance. With every day that passed the chances of a successful withdrawal grew slimmer. Guderian urged upon Dönitz the urgent need for reinforcements on the Oder. All his own previous attempts to convince Hitler of this need had been parried by the Führer with his favourite argument about the danger of Sweden entering the war at the last moment. The embassy in Sweden reported the very opposite but Hitler insisted on believing that it was only the presence of the Curland divisions which prevented Sweden from coming in. Moreover Hitler persisted in the belief, shared by Dönitz, that with the loss of Curland the important U-boat training bases in the Danzig–Gdingen –Helga area would be endangered. General Christian was still giving his report.

'Six planes were employed to supply units cut off in Budapest. In the Silesian combat area our units have had some success against enemy tanks and vehicles: twenty tanks and six hundred vehicles wiped out. The First Fighter Command has been particularly successful in this sphere. Air Force attacks on the Soviet bridgeheads this side of the Oder and enemy troop concentrations in the area of the Ninth Army . . .'

The report went on and on, giving details of enemy bombing attacks on fiercely-contested fronts, and of the flying in of supplies for isolated fighting units. Hitler interrupted impatiently: 'Göring, what is the position as regards the use of the new fighter planes?' Göring stammered in embarrassment and gestured to General Koller to take over. He, in turn, left the talking to Christian. 'Führer, there have been certain production difficulties; the railway connections and other means of transport are becoming more and more precarious. I . . . ' Hitler interrupted him again with a testy movement of the hand. 'Never mind; go on,' he said, his voice faint and hoarse.

And General Christian continued with his report. How could the new planes possibly have been ready? Whenever a new prototype was agreed and mass production begun Hitler came up with a new modification which someone or other had talked him into, forbade the use of the near-finished aircraft and ordered a new design. It had gone on like that for years, with the result that the German aircraft industry had not been able to mass-produce any really fast machine with heavy fire power. Even the *Messerschmitt* jet fighter Me 262, which was, without a doubt, superior to the Allies' jet, was banned by Hitler in 1943 because he would not, under any circumstances, take up a defensive position. He ordered instead a boost in the building of bombers and an immediate resumption of bombing attacks on England. By 1943 several German cities had been razed to the ground; the German air defence, the German fighter planes were hopelessly inferior to those of the British and the Americans, who found the occasional sorties of German fighter pilots almost no threat at all.

It was now the turn of Admiral Wagner, head of naval operations, to outline the naval situation. Grand Admiral Dönitz was standing, as before, opposite Hitler at the map-table, and next to him was his communications officer, Admiral von Puttkamer, who, since 1934, had been Hitler's naval adjutant. The report was chiefly about troop transports and the shipping of supplies between Norway, Denmark and the German ports. He mentioned the use of the cruisers *Prince Eugen*, *Lutzow* and *Scheer* as artillery support for the army units engaged in bitter fighting in the coastal area of East Prussia; he described the transportation of troops and supplies between Curland and the western Baltic ports, and finally dwelt at length on the untiring and self-sacrificing efforts of the Navy to evacuate the hundreds of thousands of refugees from East Prussia and Danzig across the sea by the few channels that remained open.

The report was over and Admiral Wagner stepped back.

Nearly everyone of rank and title present took part in the ensuing discussion, regardless of whether they had the slightest military expertise. The briefing was then officially over, but Grand Admiral Dönitz now turned once again to Hitler. All eyes were riveted on him as he began to speak:

'Führer, I should like to report on the question of the repatriation of the Curland troops. Army High Command has drawn up a plan for their withdrawal. It involves the ruthless redirection of all available shipboard space, and the strongest possible support from the *Luftwaffe*. The loading capacity of Windau and Libau are quite adequate. All in all the operation will involve about 500,000 men. I would reckon on four weeks for the withdrawal of the rank and file and the vital equipment. Some of the heavy equipment will certainly have to be abandoned.'

Dönitz pleaded with all the urgency he could muster for Guderian's plan. His own change of heart in favour of this plan resulted from the stark fact that the Russians had now got as far as the gates of Danzig and Gdynia. Hitler got up slowly and made a few sluggish turns about the room, his left leg dragging behind him, his hands crossed behind his back. Then he turned abruptly and spat his reply at Dönitz, his voice loud and harsh: 'I have already said once that a repatriation of the Curland troops is out of the question. I cannot abandon the heavy equipment: moreover I must take Sweden into account.' Then, a little more quietly, he went on: 'One division may be evacuated. Guderian, let me have a plan for this by tomorrow. I thank you gentlemen – Bormann, please stay here.' The officers saluted, the adjutants picked up their documents, and everyone except Bormann filed out of the room.

As soon as the massive doors of the operations room had

closed behind us there was a scurry of activity in the ante-room. Göring and his orderly officer left immediately, followed by Himmler, Kaltenbrunner and Fegelein. The adjutants were busy on the telephone, but everyone else sat down to take some refreshments and talk over the situation. An orderly approached General Keitel and offered him a box of cigars. He picked one out with meticulous care and, smiling contentedly, prepared ceremoniously to smoke it. A second cigar disappeared into his right-hand breast pocket. Dönitz relaxed over a glass of schnapps with his staff officers. We stayed for about half an hour in the ante-room and then retraced our steps through the long corridors, past the numberless rooms and all the sentries and security checks, until, at last, we found ourselves back in the fresh air. It was almost half past seven when our car drew up to take us back to Zossen.

It was a starry night, and we drove back through the blacked-out city of Berlin without headlights. A sea of rubble rolled past us, street after street, without a single sign of life or ray of light. Dark and eerie, like the scenery of a ghost world, the ruined remains of houses loomed up against the night sky: it was hard to believe that a flourishing metropolis with brightly lit streets, elegant window displays and fashionably dressed people had ever existed there. At one point we narrowly escaped hitting a barricade which had been hastily erected because of an unexploded bomb. But soon we left Berlin behind us and found ourselves engulfed by the piquant scent of pine woods. We drove on for about half an hour and then the car turned off to the left and through a large gateway. We had arrived at the headquarters at Zossen, about thirty kilometres south of Berlin.

These headquarters consisted of two blocks: 'Maybach II' which contained all the General Staff departments and

'Maybach I', about five hundred metres farther south, which housed the members of Army High Command and all operational staff. The bunkers had been built in a horseshoe shape in the Brandenburg forest, and were extremely well camouflaged. The entire bunker complex had been completed as early as 1939, and had served as a base for the very first German headquarters, during the Poland campaign. There were twelve bunkers, all interconnected by underground passages; two of them had two underground levels; there was also a subterranean link with 'Office 500', the largest telecommunications centre in Germany, which was buried twenty metres deep. Here all the military and vital civilian telephone lines converged, linking Central Command and the Berlin administration with the entire Reich and all of German-occupied Europe. It was called 'Zeppelin'.

We had scarcely arrived in our operations-room bunker when we were warned to expect an air-raid fairly shortly from British bombers approaching Berlin. And then, at nine o'clock, a call came through from the Reich Chancellery: 'Briefing at midnight in the Führer's bunker. Approach via Hermann-Göring-Strasse. General Gehlen is to bring his dossiers on the Hungarian and Pomeranian Fronts with him.'

Hitler frequently called these night-time conferences, showing not the slightest consideration for the rest of us. He himself had long been a night-bird, but for us these briefings were just a wearisome waste of time. It made General Guderian very angry, knowing as he did that we were all overburdened with work already. Hardly had I replaced the receiver when the Chancellery rang again. 'Because of the air-raid the briefing will take place at one o'clock; apart from this your instructions stand as before.' Another night's sleep was obviously going to be lost.

We sat out the air-raid in the deeper of the two underground levels in our bunker, and moved back upstairs when the alarm was over. These moves up and down were a complicated business because we had to take all our important documents with us. We were to return to Berlin shortly, but before leaving we had to gather as much information as we could about which parts of the city had been worst hit by the bombing raid and where the worst fires were, so that we should not be held up by the cordons.

2. ENEMY ARMIES EAST

'Maybach I' and 'Maybach II' housed, respectively, Army High Command (OKW), and German Armed Forces High Command (OKH). Above ground, all that could be seen by the casual observer was an apparently innocent one-storey house with a gabled roof. Great pains had been taken during the building of the shelters to cause as little damage to the woods as possible. It was probably due to these precautions that the two bunker systems were overlooked by Allied bombing raids.

In October 1944 I had reported for duty in the OKH. The Chief of General Staff and his department were in House 5 of the Maybach system, and the Operations Department was in House 6. House 3 contained a special department of Military Intelligence, called 'Enemy Armies East'. At that point in the war, the Chief of General Staff was Colonel-General Heinz Guderian; chief of 'Enemy Armies East' was Reinhard Gehlen, then still only a colonel; chief of the Operations Department was General Wenk. 'Enemy Armies East' was supposed to collate information from Military Intelligence and Counter-Intelligence (class 1c) concerning the eastern front. It was responsible for evaluating this information from the point of view of military tactics, for deciding on military objectives and determining their order of priority.

The methods employed by the Department might be compared with work on a complicated and intricate mosaic. Hundreds of reports from prisoners, defectors, agents and commandos who had been dropped behind the Russian Front or who had penetrated the Russian lines, reports from radio intelligence, from air reconnaissance, tactical ground reconnaissance, telephone and news media intelligence, statements collected from civilians, the evaluation of data taken from the papers of men killed in action – all these contributed to our picture of the military situation and to a knowledge of Russian military strength which was invaluable to our own troops in operations planning and decision making. Every single report was subjected to the most careful scrutiny, compared with reports from different sources, and then, with an almost pedantic attention to detail, pieced together to form the composite picture of an enemy advance or of the situation in a particular sector of the front line. Gehlen had devoted years of conscientious work to building up a comprehensive picture of Russian Armed Forces: he knew details of their various strengths, and of personnel right down to division level, sometimes even right down to regiment level; in the case of special units, he knew all about their strength in vehicles, tanks, ammunition and other equipment. In addition to this he had collected a unique body of information on the Russian armament potential, on the material support they received from the rest of the Allies and on troop morale. There was even a book we called the *Red Bible* which contained the most intimate personal details about all high-ranking Russian officers, political figures and heads of industries.

When all this information had been pieced together the work of the General Staff began. The results had to be scrutinized and processed, the military aims of the Russians on the German Front deduced and recognized and these data put at the disposal of the Operations Staff of OKH to form the basis of operational planning. Our knowledge of the dates of planned Russian attacks, of the concentrations of enemy troops and of the directions in which they would probably advance ought also to have formed the basis of Hitler's military decisions in his capacity as Supreme Commander of the Armed Forces.

When I reported for duty, I was told to report to Reinhard Gehlen. Gehlen made an immediate and lasting impression on me. He was quite different from the type of officer I had been dealing with for so long at the front. He looked more like a professor in uniform than an officer in the fifth year of the war. He was well-groomed and his lean face with its high forehead suggested intellectual refinement. His mode of speech matched his appearance. He never wasted words and whatever he said was well-considered and well-formulated. His questions were always to the point. There was nothing superfluous or muddled in his style of argument or conversation. My first interview with Gehlen must have satisfied him, for he took me, straight away, into the room where the daily briefings took place. Here several large General Staff maps were spread out, covered with blue lines and markings in red ink. Until this point I had been serving at the front throughout the war. I had had no dealings with Military Intelligence or Counter-Intelligence and was completely unacquainted with their methods.

Now I suddenly saw the war from an entirely new viewpoint. Hitherto the only military maps I had been allowed to see had contained information about the position of one battalion, one regiment, or at the very most one division; but here in front of me were maps of the whole eastern Front. Gehlen must have noticed my surprise, because he allowed me a few minutes to myself before beginning to explain the situation at the front. This again was something completely new for me, for Gehlen did not discuss the position of the German front lines, German troop strength and the material resources at the disposal of German High Command. He talked rather about the position of the Russian front lines, the massing of Russian tank divisions, about the Russian Navy and Air Force. He then outlined the general conclusions he had drawn from the position of the Russian Front, Russian troop movements and massing of tanks.

On the southern front, facing the German Army Group South, the Russians were putting increasing pressure on Budapest, moving in a north-westerly direction, that is, towards the Austrian border. Further east and north-east, high in the mountains and the northern foothills of the Carpathians, the Russians were engaged in pitched battle with the German Eighth Army, the First Hungarian Army and the First German *Panzers*. In this sector the mountain ranges of the Carpathians were providing the German and Hungarian troops with good rearguard and defensive positions. The Russians had recognized this and, compared with other sectors, were not concentrating nearly as much on the Russian Second and Fourth Ukrainian Fronts, where they faced added difficulties.

Gehlen then turned his attention to the sector of the Russian Front between the Carpathians and Warsaw. As a climax to their summer offensive, which had brought them from Mogilhev via Minsk and Brest-Litovsk as far as Warsaw, and which had been an even greater disaster for the Germans than Stalingrad, the Russians had succeeded in crossing the Vistula in three places within this sector.

Gehlen was particularly interested in these three bridge-heads, at Varka, Pulavy and Baranov, all between sixty and two hundred kilometres south of Warsaw. He pointed out to me that Russian troop activity on the First Ukrainian and First White Russian Fronts was greatly in excess of the norm and had reached proportions only compatible with major

60

battle situations. He touched on one or two other eastern fronts and then, noticing my consternation, he added, 'I'm afraid that's the way things are going out there, right now.'

My first lesson over, Lieutenant Wessel, Gehlen's Chief-of-Staff, introduced me to my new colleagues, and showed me which sector of the Russian Front was to be my special responsibility. It was the sector to which Gehlen had paid particular attention in his lecture, the stretch between the Carpathians and the point at which the Narev joins the Vistula; it contained the three Russian bridgeheads at Varka, Pulavy and Baranov. Our front line in this sector was formed by German Army Group Central with the Fourth *Panzers* and the Ninth and Seventeenth Armies.

What I had heard and seen on my first day at High Command kept me awake that night until the small hours. During all my years at the front I had never had time to feel helpless or at a loss as to what to do next, even in desperate situations with the odds heavily against us, because the heat of battle and the struggle for survival had absorbed all my attention and energies. But the situation was entirely different here. I no longer had a part to play; I was no more than a mere observer. It was very difficult indeed to come to terms with this unaccustomed state of affairs, and I succumbed to the deepest depression of my life. During the next few days, before I officially took up my new duties, I took part in conferences, listened to lectures on the military situation and generally familiarized myself with the work. Gehlen summoned me once again to give me a further run-down on the Russian strike potential and listed the forces we still had left at our disposal. He once again gravely emphasized the importance of the three Russian bridgeheads, prophesying that the fate of the entire eastern front would probably be decided there during the course of the winter. The information collected by his department so far had all pointed to the fact that the Russians had wasted no time after their initial successes in crossing the Vistula at Varka, Pulavy and Baranov and had immediately brought up reinforcements and taken up a defensive position. All attempts on our part to sweep these three bridgeheads away had failed, simply because we had not thrown enough men into the attack. The Russians had even succeeded in bettering their positions in some places and, during the weeks and months following their summer offensive, in extending the bridgeheads slightly to the west.

In June the Allies had made a successful landing on the coast of Normandy. For months now the battle being waged there had proved exhausting for German fighting potential and had forced us to direct all available forces to that theatre, particularly the *élite* of our *Panzer* divisions. Stalin's constant demands for a second front in France had ensured that German High Command could not withdraw enough troops to push the Russians back across the Vistula and use the river as the backbone of a really strong German line of defence.

The impressive and impassioned way in which Gehlen explained to me the situation on the eastern Front demonstrated the conflict, perhaps even the tragedy, of his role at the head of Military Intelligence. He devoted all his energies uncompromisingly to reconnaissance work against the Russians, although he knew that Hitler did not recognize the value of his information and would not act on his recommendations. He was by no means a devoted follower of Hitler, quite the reverse, but as a soldier he was passionately committed to reconnaissance and intelligence work against the Russians.

Our daily routine in the 'Enemy Armies East' Department, like the routine of every other department of the General Staff, was conditioned by 'Hitler's briefing', at which representatives of all three armed forces were expected to report to Hitler every morning. Our representative was General Guderian. He prepared himself for this military briefing with one of his own, the 'Chief of General Staff Briefing', thus ensuring that he was sufficiently informed of the latest developments to be able to advise the Führer and also to make his own decisions and run his own department. This meeting took place at eleven o'clock every morning, and since Gehlen was one of those expected to appear with the latest reports, he, in turn, held his own briefing at ten o'clock, when the various section leaders gave him a run-down on their own sectors. We had to be at work by seven o'clock in the morning in order to have it ready in time. Reports from our Army Group, on enemy activity during the night, had to be processed and entered on maps which were kept up to date with information on Russian army units, troop movements and any other important details. We also consulted the relevant department of the *Luftwaffe* and other sections for information that had been passed to them during the night, and entered it all on the map.

Reconnaissance at the front was carried out by scout patrols and shock-troops, by means of restricted, probing attacks, and even by noting sounds and gauging the direction from which they came. Prisoners and deserters were interrogated and civilians questioned, enemy transmissions were monitored and the Russian telephone network tapped by special units, either directly or by means of shunt connections. Specialists from the Brandenburg Division or agents from the special training centre of 'Enemy Armies East' were parachuted behind enemy lines, where they carried out special missions and were then picked up again by front-line troops. Intelligence units of the 'Enemy Armies East' Department and of the SS sent in radio reports on the transportation of troops and material out of the Russian hinterland and also on factories producing machines and other material vital to the war effort. *Luftwaffe* short-range reconnaissance planes provided us with aerial photographs of the front and of Russian-held territory well behind the front lines, giving us vital information on Russian troop movements and concentrations, rail transports, vehicle convoys, bridge and road construction, airfields, artillery positions, tank concentrations and various other useful items. It all formed a complex and colourful jigsaw puzzle, which it was our task to assemble piece by piece. Sometimes we received false information, but we usually recognized it as such pretty quickly, simply because it did not fit into our nice, neat jigsaw puzzle. During the course of the Russian War, almost every major Russian troop concentration and preparation for major offensives was recognized and reported by Gehlen's department on the basis of information gathered in this way.

Hitler, however, was not to be convinced of the value of these methods and the results they produced, even though Gehlen had the support of the highest-ranking officers, all of whom had been trained at General Staff and knew that fighting a war without reconnaissance work was impossible. Hitler considered himself a military genius and had been encouraged in this belief by his initial successes. He could not tolerate the idea that anything should influence his free and inspired master-minding of vast tactical plans. This was one of the reasons for our grave military reverses and the final catastrophic defeat of our eastern campaign.

In major battle situations, that is, during major Russian offensives, Gehlen's department was exceptionally busy. A second daily briefing was held in the evenings, so that information could be passed on even more quickly than usual. This meant that we had to work right up to the evening briefing, and as there was always work to do afterwards, I was kept at my desk until the early hours of the morning.

I was entirely dependent on the telephone so that when, during major offensives, lines were overloaded, blocked or even destroyed, the situation was almost impossible, particularly during the day. Front-line troops were on the move and had no time to process reports and pass them on, so I had to take the initiative and try to collect information from any other source that offered. At night, however, there were fewer difficulties. We did not have to rely on bald factual reports which somehow lacked conviction; we could check our information through personal conversations and get a much better general picture of the situation at the front for the next morning's briefing.

During the months of October, November and December, 1944, my work was dominated by the three bridgeheads; the number of reports from these areas increased daily. While Hitler was gathering together two armies, containing some of our best officers and supplemented by the larger part of our *Panzer* divisions, in the hope that a last mighty effort would turn the tables in the west, the Russians were concentrating troops along the eastern front in hitherto unprecedented numbers. By the beginning of November we had an astonishingly clear picture of Russian resources, concentration, plans, etc., on the basis of material gathered and processed. The Russian units observed at the Baranov bridgehead and in the area round it on the eastern bank of the Vistula proved to us beyond all possible doubt that Marshall Konyev was stationed there with his First Ukrainian Front – all too familiar to us – waiting for reinforcements and preparing to attack the industrial area of Upper Silesia. At the Pulavy and Varka bridgeheads Marshall Zhukov was mustering his First White Russian Front, which had a deservedly high reputation

65

as being a very tough body of men. His thrust westwards could only be aimed at the heart of Germany, at Berlin itself.

Drawn up against this troop concentration of two Russian armies in the two hundred kilometres between Warsaw and the bend in the Vistula, was the German Army Group Central, considerably weakened by the Russian summer offensive of 1944, though reinforced by the Ninth and the Fourth *Panzers*. News from these areas during the first half of November left no room for doubt that troop movements and preparations for battle were by no means completed, but that the Russians were bringing up yet further troops, materials and ammunition. The numbers and designations of entirely new infantry, armoured divisions, artillery or air-force divisions appeared almost daily in the reports. The number of deserters was unexpectedly, in fact astonishingly, light and many civilians were on the move from the Russian hinterland to behind the German lines, from whom we were able to obtain a very clear picture of Russian troop movements. Reports received from the three bridgehead areas gave such incredibly high figures for the Russian strength accumulated there, that it was decided to employ all available resources to confirm or disprove these reports. None of the reconnaissance checks carried out over a period of some two weeks produced any results which varied materially from our previous information; on the contrary the impression of the situation we had received at the beginning of November was substantiated more and more firmly from day to day.

As far as I was concerned the result of this development was that I could no longer get through all the work that had to be done during the day, and so I worked through most of the night as well. Gehlen would appear almost every night about midnight armed with a coffee pot, lend a hand with

66

whatever we were doing and give us some valuable advice. Occasionally he picked up the telephone and got in touch with officers he knew whose units were drawn up against the Russian concentration zone. Gehlen's unreserved friendliness and constant assistance during this period of stress endeared him to me greatly.

One night, it must have been the end of November or right at the beginning of December, he started up a long conversation during the course of which he informed me that air-force reconnaissance and reliable agents had warned us to expect the Russian troops drawn up and making ready east of the Vistula to move shortly into the bridgehead areas. For the first time the date 10–15 January was proposed for the expected Russian offensive. But we were still not entirely sure that the Russians weren't deliberately trying to mislead us, while planning the attack for December. The speed of their troop concentration at the bridgeheads seemed to suggest as much. Gehlen also mentioned a third possibilty, that the Russians were simply trying to avoid the difficulties of supply and transport which might arise if the ice on the Vistula broke up early and started to drift.

'I need every detail you can give me, even the most insignificant, if I am to work out the true date of the offensive as quickly as possible. Once we know that, we can add it to our information on Russian strength to convince Hitler that reinforcements, *Panzers* and artillery in particular, *must* be sent to strengthen Army Group Central. Otherwise there will be a terrible catastrophe – you can't imagine how terrible. Army Group Central has far too few troops in the front line and only one single division in reserve!'

Hitler was already familiar with the situation in this area. He had been kept constantly informed of it by General

Guderian, who respected Gehlen's work very highly, and by Gehlen himself, both in personal interviews and written reports. Yet, despite this overwhelming and dismaying evidence from the bridgeheads, Hitler was not prepared to go so far as to reinforce Army Group Central even with infantry divisions, so that the front could, at last, be more realistically manned for defence. At present the divisions were covering sectors that were unjustifiably long. Instead, Hitler sent every available army unit, and all our reserves of *Panzers* and materials to the west.

16 December 1944 arrived, the day on which Hitler began his last major offensive in the west, in the Ardennes. The younger officers, including myself, were very impressed by our successes during the first few days. Gehlen, on the other hand, was not so easily impressed. In a conversation which took place shortly before Christmas he said casually, 'What's the point of all this, anyway? The *Panzer* divisions fighting there are desperately needed on the Vistula, to save Silesia, Pomerania, East Prussia, West Prussia and probably even Berlin from imminent Russian attack.'

Reports received from mid-December onwards confirmed that the Russian offensive would not begin until January after all, and could be expected between 12 and 15 January. Between Christmas and New Year Gehlen again took a personal hand in my work. We discussed the few remaining sources of information on the sectors in the greatest danger and put our plans into action. Guderian had to make his special appointment to talk to Hitler once again on 31 December and he intended to take Gehlen with him to the 'Eagle's Eyrie' headquarters.

Gehlen was only too well aware of the difficulties he would encounter in trying to make Hitler act on his information. It was difficult enough even to get him to listen to it. As this interview was so desperately important, he decided to employ a device which was to say the least unusual for an officer of the General Staff. The latest figures from the areas of Russian concentration were checked and rechecked. Then Gehlen also collected the latest figures from the Operations Department of German High Command on our own troop strength in the threatened areas. Under Gehlen's direction I drew up the maps to be shown to Hitler – marking everything to scale on both sides, showing the relative troop strengths in the area and demonstrating the Russian military superiority in infantry, armoured divisions, artillery, air arm and materials. When we had finished, small blue German soldiers and large red Russian soldiers faced each other on either side of the front line, backed up by small blue German *Panzers* and large red Russian tanks, small blue armaments stock-piles and large red stock-piles. This was repeated with every other item and beside each blue or red figure we entered the exact figures, so that we could not be accused of flashy superficiality or of trying to mislead Hitler by optical illusions. In many positions the ratio was 1:10 in troops and even more unfavourable for us as regards tanks and materials; so the maps were extremely impressive and convincing.

The outcome of the interview was a shattering disappointment for everyone connected with Gehlen's work. Hitler showed no interest whatever in our information. He finally yielded to Guderian's relentless pressure only to the extent of ordering two companies into the area as mobile reserves for Army Group Central. Gehlen returned from this interview with Hitler more depressed than ever. Hitler had hardly noticed his specially prepared material, let alone used it as a basis for any decisions. The fate of the German Front between the Carpathians and East Prussia was allowed to take its course.

On 1 January 1945 Gehlen invited his officers over for a few drinks. Whether he was prompted to do this to celebrate his long-overdue promotion, by a spirit of resignation after his interview with Hitler, or simply the feeling that he would like to confide in his staff, I cannot say. He gave a speech in honour of the New Year, dwelling first on the military and political developments of the past twelve months, thanking all his colleagues for their work and their support. Then, somewhat rashly, he gave us his own frank preview of the coming year.

Gehlen predicted that the war on our eastern front would be over by April or May 1945 at the latest. He based this judgement on the fact that the Russians were now much stronger than we were, both from a military and an economic point of view and that our situation was deteriorating rapidly. Since we were fighting a war on two fronts, we had no hope of offering resistance to the Russians for any length of time: our resources in all fields were fast dwindling and the people were exhausted and without hope. The vast material superiority of the Western Allies on land and in the air and in reserves of all kinds meant that our chances in the west were even worse than in the east. Gehlen did not conceal the fact that he thought there was no point in carrying on hostilities against the Western Allies. He concluded by saying that in his opinion all the German troops should be removed from the western Front, regardless of the consequences and thrown into the struggle against the Russians. Our first objective should be to ensure that Central Europe's eastern front should not be pushed any farther westwards by the Russians than could possibly be helped. He touched on the coming Yalta Conference at which, he said, the fate of Germany and her people would be decided by the Allies. When Gehlen had finished speaking, there was silence for some time.

No one had the heart for cheerful conversation any more, and we soon silently dispersed.

The reports we received during the first days of January confirmed the dates Gehlen had foreseen for the offensive. The Russians had massed troops at the bridgeheads in quite unbelievable numbers. The figures given for the artillery and ammunition especially, were beyond anything we had estimated, and it was plain that this was a quite unprecedented concentration. The situation was so perilous that High Command decided that General von Saucken's *Panzer* group, which had at last been sent to reinforce Army Group Central in January, should be held in reserve far enough behind the front line to be safe from the heavy Russian fire expected immediately before the offensive. Command also hoped by this decision to keep the *Panzers* mobile for employment where there was greatest need. When Hitler heard of this decision he gave the order that they should be drawn up from three to six kilometres behind the front line: this meant that they were in the direct line of fire, well within Russian artillery range. He did not give any reasons for this order and there was no time to have his decision reversed, as the Russian offensive was imminent.

12 January arrived and with it Marshal Konyev's attack from the Baranov bridgehead.

On 13 January Marshal Zhukov began his offensive from the Pulavy and Varka bridgeheads. General von Saucken's *Panzer* corps drawn up in reserve bore the brunt of the heavy Russian artillery fire which lasted some hours and prepared the way for the attack. Everyone in the department worked day and night to the point of physical exhaustion. A few hours after their artillery opened fire, Russian troops were streaming over the bridgeheads like water pouring in torrents through a breached dam, for all the world as if there had

71

never been a German Front at all. They pushed rapidly westwards, often entirely disregarding or bypassing German units, which soon found themselves completely surrounded like islands in a stream. The Russians' only aim was to reach Germany without delay.

Gehlen spent nearly every day working with us at this time. But it was too late for Military Intelligence to be of any use. The front lines had collapsed, their command posts were destroyed, their officers captured or on the move, searching for safer positions farther westward. Events at the front moved so quickly that our communications with the active troops were cut for days and we had no idea of the latest developments. Large troop formations, with whom we had hitherto maintained constant contact, seemed to disappear completely for days at a time. Hitler did, finally, send rail transports of reserves into this storm from the east, but when they reached their destinations they found they were already behind the Russian lines. By the fifth and sixth days of the Russian offensive Konyev's advance troops had reached the edge of the Upper Silesian industrial belt, and on the tenth day Glogau on the Oder.

On 20 January I had to leave my post in Gehlen's department and join General Guderian, who had appointed me his aide. One last service I was able to perform for Gehlen was to move his family from Saxony to Bavaria. Gehlen already knew that the Yalta Conference had decided that the Russians would retain control of Saxony at the end of the war. After that I saw the General almost daily at Guderian's briefings until both Generals were relieved of their responsibilities by Hitler and the 'Enemy Armies East' Department was disbanded.

Shortly after midnight on that February night when we

had been summoned back to a further meeting with Hitler we set off towards a horizon lit by the distant glare of fire. Soon we were turning slowly out of the Hermann-Göring-Strasse into the narrow road leading to the Führer's bunker. The security arrangements were doubly strict at night. On every corner there were sentries armed with sub-machine-guns and hand grenades. We were escorted by one of them from the car park to the bunker entrance and there handed over to another.

The whole bunker construction in the garden of the Reich Chancellery was only begun in 1944, when the shelters and cellars directly beneath the Chancellery itself proved too flimsy to provide adequate protection for Hitler and his close associates. The underground installation in the garden was therefore begun in a great hurry and was never properly finished off. It consisted of two storeys: the lower storey, something like sixteeen metres below the ground, contained Hitler's rooms, including the conference room where our nocturnal briefing was to take place.

We descended what seemed like countless steps, between bare, cold, concrete walls. At the bottom we met the same SS officers who had checked our papers that afternoon. Once again we had to lay down our weapons and coats and try to look pleasant and inoffensive while the guards ran a trained eye over us. We were allowed to proceed to the ante-room, where Guderian was greeted by Kaltenbrunner. We were told that Hitler was once again closeted with Bormann, and we waited a few minutes before the door opened and Bormann asked Kaltenbrunner to come in. I watched Kaltenbrunner go, trying to analyse the curiously strong antipathy I had always felt towards him. Perhaps his physiognomy had something to do with it: his features were coarse and brutish; if his duelling scars had not betrayed the former student one would have taken him for a labourer of some sort. He was six feet tall, with remarkably broad shoulders and clawlike hands – whenever he shook hands with me I worried about my hand. An Austrian by birth, he owed his successful career to his political fanaticism, ice-cold ruthlessness and love of intrigue.

He was head of the Reich Security Central Office (*Reichssicher heitshauptamt*), which combined the criminal police and the political police, or Gestapo, under one administration. His elevation to power had come with the assassination of Heydrich. During the period between Hitler's seizure of power and the beginning of the war, Himmler's deputy, SS *Obergruppenführer* Heydrich, had succeeded in making Himmler heavily dependent on him. It was an open secret in Berlin at the time that Heydrich always got his way with Himmler. But in the early years of the war some of the other men on Himmler's staff, Schellenberg and Ohlendorf in particular, managed to denigrate Heydrich in Himmler's eyes so that his influence was somewhat eroded. However, he managed all the same to gain increasing sway over Hitler himself and even to wring out of the Führer the post of Reich's Protector in Bohemia-Moravia. Then, in 1943, Heydrich was shot by Czech resistance fighters. Himmler was faced with the task of replacing him as head of Reich Security, and this time he was determined not to appoint anyone who might repeat Heydrich's feat of rising from the ranks of his own staff to become a dangerous rival to *Reichsführer* Himmler himself. So he appointed Kaltenbrunner who was, at the time, head of the criminal police and the Gestapo in Vienna.

For a time Kaltenbrunner played safe and allowed himself to be Himmler's willing tool. Then he too began to intrigue on his own account. His ambition made use of the mutual loathing which existed between the three men who made a practice of currying favour with Hitler: Goebbels, Himmler and Bormann. (Göring was another member of this group but his prestige had suffered so much as a result of the disappointing *Luftwaffe* performance that he was no longer a front runner.) Each of these men plotted constantly to drive his rivals from the field, so that it was a serious threat to Bormann's position when Himmler was appointed an Army Group Commander in 1944 and began to concentrate more and more openly on building up his own military power. Bormann found Kaltenbrunner a useful stooge. Slowly and discreetly he edged him into Hitler's notice, a manoeuvre which was made all the easier for him by Himmler's new Army post, which compelled him to spend most of his time with the Army, establishing his military efficiency. Kaltenbrunner had already risen so high in Hitler's estimation that the Führer now gave orders directly to him, without conveying them through Himmler in the normal way.

My thoughts were interrupted by the appearance of Hitler, Bormann and Kaltenbrunner together. We exchanged brief greetings and then filed into the conference room. It was a small, bare place, with grey-painted walls, containing only a brown bench set against one wall, a large map-table and a desk chair. There were very few people present, and Hitler immediately asked Guderian to report on the situation in the east. Guderian took full advantage of this rare opportunity and launched into another desperate plea for his plan to check the Soviet advance. He spoke in a harsh, emphatic tone, beginning with the central theme of the immediate threat to Berlin. He stressed that with Berlin all of Germany would stand or fall: he spoke of the need to keep open the door of escape for millions of German refugees from the east, and of Stalin's order giving Soviet troops, as they advanced, three days' licence to murder, rape and plunder. He insisted that one more attempt must be made to ward off this danger and to gain time.

After a short silence Hitler asked, in a cold, expressionless voice, about the strength of the Russian spearhead advancing towards Berlin. General Gehlen supplied the information that in terms of troops the Russians were about five times as strong as the Germans, and with regard to tanks, artillery and ammunition supplies the ratio was much more unfavourable to the German armies. Gehlen began to lay out his maps to demonstrate this crushing Russian superiority more clearly, but Hitler brushed him aside.

At this point Guderian plunged ahead with his plan for Pomerania, describing it again in minute detail: he stressed once more the hopelessness of our situation and the urgent necessity of this final plan; the immediate extrication of the two Curland armies; the massing of absolutely all available reserves within the Reich and Italy for immediate transfer to Pomerania; the redirection from the Ardennes of the Sixth SS Armoured Division under Sepp Dietrich (the strongest German armoured unit), regardless of any weakening of the western front. With this fighting force of thirty to forty divisions and about 1,500 tanks, Guderian intended to mount attacks southwards from Pomerania and north-eastwards from the area around Glogau. He hoped, by this means, to avert the immediate threat to Berlin and to establish a strong line of defence along the border fortifications on the old German-Polish frontier known as the *Tirschtigel* position. Everything was to be wagered on this one last card. Guderian was talking passionately now, paying no heed to Hitler's dismissive gestures. To substantiate his plan he thrust under Hitler's nose maps, diagrams and calculations drawn up by General Gehlen and his staff from air reconnaissance, intelligence reports and the statements of prisoners and deserters.

Hitler remained quite silent, staring blankly at the maps with his hands clasped together. Guderian was exhausted; he looked towards Hitler for a reply but for a while there was no response at all. The silence grew more and more oppressive, interrupted only by the occasional muffled thud of exploding incendiary bombs. I held my breath while the fate of the German east was being decided. Hitler stood up slowly, limped a few paces and stared into space. Suddenly he stopped still and dismissed us quickly and coldly, without passing a single word of comment on the urgent plea he had heard. Only Bormann stayed behind. The last die was cast.

3. THE GENERALS AND HITLER'S MEN

Hitler ignored the suggestions of his General Staff in reaching his decisions. So little faith, in fact, did he have in their advice, that late in March 1945 he discharged Guderian and reduced Gehlen's 'Enemy Armies East' department of Military Intelligence to a mere rump, incapable of effective work. The twenty-two divisions of the Sixteenth and Eighteenth Armies stayed in Curland. The Sixth SS *Panzer* Army from the Ardennes and some other divisions from the western front and from Italy were transferred to Hungary, and not to Pomerania, where the German troops were engaged in a vain struggle against far superior numbers. In the area between Lake Balaton and Budapest, around Stuhlweissenberg, twelve hundred tanks were collected for an assault which was totally senseless in view of the situation at the gates of Berlin. Here in Hungary the Sixth Army and the Sixth *Panzer* Army under Sepp Dietrich (together forming the Balk Army Group), a cavalry corps and parts of the Third Hungarian Army were assembled. Hitler's idea was to attack to the south and east with these forces, in order to regain the area from Pécs to the junction of the Danube and the Drava, to slot Budapest back into the German system of defences, and to make the Danube up to the influx of the Drava the backbone of the German defences in Hungary. The offensive in Pomerania, on the other hand, was launched only by parts of the frail Third *Panzer* Army and parts of the Eleventh Army with not more than about five hundred tanks altogether.

Guderian had not given way easily. Even in early March

he was still trying, using General Gehlen's detailed calculations of the enemy strength and position, to dissuade Hitler from his plans. The only result of these efforts, however, was that both of them, Guderian and Gehlen, made themselves more and more unpopular with Hitler. There was one occasion in particular, when Gehlen was delivering a report on the situation, during which he once again offered conclusive facts, worked out with expert precision, about Soviet intentions and troop concentrations. Hitler declared imperiously and with a great show of emotion: 'I utterly reject these puerile offerings from the General Staff. It takes a genius to recognize the enemy's intentions and then to draw the conclusions necessary for leadership. And no genius would ever bother with such mechanical pedantry.'

Things got so bad that whenever Guderian or Gehlen presented Hitler with unpalatable news or facts, he would forbid them to address him 'in such a one-sided and biased way'. More than once he even said that he must follow his own instinct for military leadership quite uninfluenced by others, obeying only his inspiration. There were few occasions when Hitler's instinct to dominate gave way. It happened once, towards the end, when I was still accompanying Guderian to conferences.

The date was 12 March 1945. The conference in the Reich Chancellery began as usual at 4 pm. Once reports on the situations in the east and the west had been given, as well as reports by the *Luftwaffe* and the Navy, everybody taking part in the conference left the room, with the exception of Guderian and Bormann, who were requested to stay with Hitler. Guderian kept me back too, with the papers covering the eastern front. Hitler was expecting *Panzer* General Dietrich von Saucken, who was to be briefed on his new command immediately after the conference. On 19 March von Saucken was commissioned by Hitler to lead the Second Army Group, which was fighting in the area of Danzig, Gdynia and the Vistula delta. It was entirely dependent on its own resources, except for a tenuous link across the Frische Nehrung with the vestiges of the Fourth Army, and otherwise quite cut off from the rest of Germany.

In 1939 von Saucken had set out from East Prussia to fight in Poland as a cavalryman. Later on, when the German armoured forces expanded, he had to exchange his horse for a tank, and with his former cavalry troopers he had become the leader of one of the best armoured units in the Army. Von Saucken had not distinguished himself again until the end of January and beginning of February 1945, when, with his tank corps, he successfully fought his way back from the smashed Vistula Front in the rear of the victorious Russian assault units, and reached the Oder near Steinau. Early in February von Saucken crossed the Oder with his corps and on 4 February joined the German defences. Von Saucken held the Knight's Cross with oak leaves and swords.

Günsche, Hitler's personal adjutant, came in and announced the arrival of *Panzer* General von Saucken. We were standing beside Hitler, who was seated at the map-table, when von Saucken came in. Slim, elegant, his left hand resting casually on his cavalry sabre, his monocle in his eye, von Saucken saluted and gave a slight bow. This was three 'outrages' at once. He had not given the Nazi salute with raised arm and the words 'Heil Hitler', as had been regulation since 20 July 1944, he had not surrendered his weapon on entering the operations room, and he had kept his monocle in his eye when saluting Hitler. I looked back and forth from Hitler to von Saucken, expecting something terrible to happen. Guderian and Bormann too were standing as if turned to stone. But nothing happened, nothing at all!

Hitler very briefly asked Guderian to inform von Saucken about the military position in East Prussia and the Danzig area, where von Saucken was to take over the Second Army Group. When Guderian had finished, Hitler began to speak. He developed Guderian's remarks, with some digressions, and gave von Saucken instructions about the battle which he and the Second Army Group were to fight.

Von Saucken listened in silence to all Guderian's and Hitler's remarks. He was standing right beside Hitler at the map-table. After a short pause, as if to take a deep breath, Hitler continued. He indicated to General von Saucken that in the battle area in and around Danzig he would have to accept the authority of *Gauleiter* Forster and that his, von Saucken's, duties would be confined to purely military matters. The ultimate responsibility and power of command for this whole area was to be retained by *Gauleiter* Albert Forster. Hitler paused and looked up at von Saucken as if inviting comment. The latter stiffened, returned Hitler's gaze with his monocle in his eye and, striking the marble slab of the map-table with the flat of his hand, he replied: 'I have no intention, Herr Hitler, of placing myself under the orders of a *Gauleiter*!' One could have heard a pin drop on the carpet. It seemed to me that Hitler shrank physically from the General's words. His face looked even more waxen, his body more bowed than ever.

Guderian was the first to break the leaden silence, urging von Saucken to be sensible in an admonishing, comradely tone. Even Bormann joined in. But General von Saucken's only reply was, 'I have no intention whatsoever of doing so.' Guderian and Bormann could think of nothing further to say. It seemed that the silence which followed would never end. Then Hitler answered, in a weak, expressionless voice: 'All right, Saucken, keep the command to yourself.' A few

81

more trifling matters followed. Hitler dismissed the General, without shaking his hand, and von Saucken left the room with the merest hint of a bow.

In the final weeks Hitler lost not only his powers of resistance but also much of his former decisiveness and intellectual energy. This may have been because he, like others, was not equal to the terrible strain, but it may also have resulted from the continual use of drugs. At any rate it was obvious that it was not only his body which was showing symptoms of breakdown, but his mind as well. The shaking of his head and the trembling of the left side of his body, which was especially apparent in his arm and hand, were increasing. His movements had become still more shambling, his posture more bent. When walking he would place his right hand on his left and when sitting he would cross his right leg over his left, in order to conceal the trembling of his limbs from others not in the know. He grew vacillating and indecisive to an increasing extent. At the beginning of March, for example, twenty-two pursuit tanks were to be sent by the quickest route to support the troops fighting in the Rhineland. Owing to the absolute air superiority of the Allies and to the extensive destruction of the rail network such a venture was no longer a matter of hours, but days. At first Hitler ordered that the tanks be sent to the Pirmasens area; then, when the situation on the Moselle steadily deteriorated, he revised the order to 'the Trier area'. When they failed to arrive there on time, they were diverted in the direction of Coblenz. Hitler then ordered still more detours, until finally nobody had any idea where the tanks really were. The result was that they never reached the front but fell instead into the hands of the Americans, in as good a condition as when they had left the factory.

The Russians were already on the near side of the Oder,

close enough to threaten Berlin, when Hitler ordered that preparations be made to transfer the entire headquarters to Central Germany. Parts of the government and the military leadership were to be accommodated near the Army training ground at Ohrdruf in Thuringia. But the American troops who crossed the Rhine west of Darmstadt reached this area – 'Olga headquarters' – with their advanced motorized units much sooner than the German leaders. Advance detachments and intelligence staff had to break off work hurriedly and move to 'Serail', the name given to the Berchtesgaden area, which Hitler had in the meantime designated as the new site of the headquarters. All superfluous material, files and inessential staff were sent off there in the hope that they could be recovered at some later stage. But when the Russians broke out of Hungary deeper and deeper into Austria and Bohemia, when Vienna had fallen and there was no further room for any possible doubt about the collapse of the Oder Front protecting Berlin, Hitler abandoned the 'Serail' plan again and looked towards Schleswig-Holstein. Eventually Hitler stayed put in Berlin with a small command staff, totally unprepared, lacking particularly means of communication and other facilities necessary for directing operations.

Advance American armoured units were already west of Magdeburg and in the neighbourhood of Dessau-Aken, when there was some discussion at one of the conferences as to whether the bridges on the Elbe should be blown up, particularly the valuable and strategically important Autobahn bridge. Hitler vacillated. Three timees I had to pass his orders about this to the relevant fortress section in the Army High Command, and twice I had to retract them. Each time a whole chain of command was alerted, reaching all the way to those on the spot at the bridges. In the end nobody knew what their orders really were and what was really to be done.

The fighting dragged on, creating ever greater havoc. Bridges were blown up, village after village and town after town was turned into rubble and ashes. Anything which had survived the bombs was reduced to debris by shellfire. Germany was losing an irreplaceable cultural inheritance. But the idea of giving up this senseless struggle still did not seem to enter Adolf Hitler's head. One example may serve to show the state of his mind on the subject.

When the Americans were approaching Münster in Westphalia, Cardinal Galen drove out to meet them to surrender the city. The Cardinal was an uncompromising opponent of the Nazis, who had never shrunk from sharp overt criticism of the excesses of the Nazi régime, undeterred by threats of any kind. He wanted only to save human lives and preserve the few remaining cultural treasures in the city from certain destruction. The news of the capitulation of Münster was contained in a report conveyed to Hitler in the ante-room to the conference room in his bunker, where he was just greeting those present. I was standing only a few feet away from him. His face turned into a rage-distorted grimace. In a frenzy of hate he burst out: 'If I ever lay hands on that swine, I'll have him hanged.'

Internal clashes in Hitler's inner circle continued as before. Whilst the battle for the East Prussian border was still going on, Guderian had issued an order dealing with the training and operation of the home guard (*Volkssturm*). Bormann regarded this order as trespassing on his territory. Violent clashes ensued, and Guderian had to give way. A short time later another dispute again arose between these two, this time over the Nazi leadership officers who were attached to every unit after the assassination attempt on 20 July. They were a near equivalent to the Political Commissars in the

Red Army, responsible for the general political 'supervision' of the soldiers, but chiefly of the officers. Some of these Nazi leadership officers chose this moment to get in touch with Bormann direct and report to him about 'the defeatist attitude of the officer corps in the Army Group in Silesia'. The allegations, which were not even checked, were exaggerated in both their scope and the form which they took. Bormann of course wasted no time in passing this on to Hitler, who immediately took Guderian to task about it. Guderian then wrote a sharp note to Bormann, saying that he would not tolerate interference from him in matters which did not concern him, and he ordered that the Nazi officers, who had reported direct to Bormann be severely disciplined, because they had not gone through the proper military channels. They were, in fact, subject to the direct authority of the Army and not of the Party.

Waffen SS General Fegelein, Himmler's permanent representative at Hitler's headquarters, was at the centre of another storm involving Guderian. Fegelein's behaviour towards older, distinguished military officers and government officials was marked by an offensive arrogance and uncouthness. Although he was only about thirty-seven years old, he interrupted everybody, regardless of rank and age, even when what he had to offer by way of comment or criticism was complete nonsense. In March 1945 Guderian was outlining the situation in Pomerania at a conference when Fegelein interrupted him, saying that Guderian's facts and figures were all lies and waving around a piece of paper on which a few typed figures could be read. Afterwards it emerged that all these figures were completely wrong.

But the most significant of these personal dramas involved Göring, who in increasing measure was made to feel that Hitler no longer trusted him. For some weeks Göring had appeared in a *Luftwaffe* uniform without decorations. In view of the circumstances he seemed to consider it appropriate to substitute a simpler form of dress for the pale blue buckskin uniform with red high-topped boots of Russian leather, golden spurs and indescribable headgear or other garish accessories in which he used regularly to appear. His interest in things military also seemed to be flagging more and more. Previously during situation conferences he had leant on the table and across the map with the whole breadth of his body, so that anyone standing behind him could see absolutely nothing. In the middle of a talk by Guderian or Jodl he would move his fat fingers over the map and try to give emphasis to his views, even when they revealed a total absence of military expertise. On one occasion I witnessed the climax of Göring's bad manners at a night-time conference in Hitler's bunker. We were standing round the map-table in the small conference room; Göring was the only one sitting opposite Hitler. The table was covered with big General Staff maps. Göring ostentatiously showed his boredom, yawning continuously in apparently genuine fatigue. In the end he got fed up with the whole business; he picked up his green morocco brief-case, rested his elbows on the table and buried his plump head in the soft leather. Hitler didn't seem to notice him at all. Göring may very well have been asleep by the time Hitler asked him quietly, almost softly in fact, to move his elbows, as the map on top had to be pulled away.

But during one particular conference in the Chancellery, while General Christian was reporting on the situation in the air, Hitler suddenly interrupted him in the middle of a sentence with the familiar nonsensical enquiry about how many of the latest type of fighter had come off the assembly line. Christian tried to duck the issue, but from his excuse

86

it emerged only too clearly that not a single new aircraft was airborne. For a moment Hitler was silent. Then his fists clenched convulsively, red blotches appeared on his pale face, and biting his lower lip he looked across at Göring, incensed with rage: 'Göring, your *Luftwaffe* is no longer worth keeping as an independent branch of the Armed Forces.' Vicious insults followed. Hitler threatened to dissolve the entire *Luftwaffe* and merge it with the Army. He completely lost control of himself and went so far as to threaten Göring, in the presence of us all, with degradation to the rank of Private and with drafting into the infantry at the front. He treated the Reich Marshal like a schoolboy. Finally, when Hitler had quietened down again, Göring withdrew into the ante-room and hurriedly downed a few brandies. As so often when Hitler was in a bad mood, one person after another disappeared from the conference room into the ante-room, to avoid being the next to invoke the anger of their powerful master. If further questions were raised, adjutants or orderlies had to fetch back their skulking chiefs.

In addition to everything else March 1945 was a month of personnel problems. It was difficult to find suitable commanders to continue the war. During one conference Guderian reminded Hitler of Field-Marshal von Manstein and suggested his reinstatement. Manstein with his Eleventh Army had captured Sebastopol and been one of the most successful commanders in the southern sector of the eastern front. He had also played a decisive part as a member of the General Staff in drawing up the plans for the successful major offensives at the outset of the war. But he made the 'unpardonable mistake' of warning Hitler repeatedly about the way he was conducting the war in the east. When Guderian now suggested von Manstein again, Hitler replied: 'If I had forty magnificently equipped assault divisions which could deal the enemy a decisive blow, von Manstein would be the only possible choice as commander of these troops. He is probably the most able officer to emerge from the ranks of the present General Staff. In the situation as it now stands, however, he is of no use to me. He has no faith in National Socialism. He is therefore unable to stand up to the stresses which a general faces in the German military situation of today.'

It was in March too that the collapse of the Lake Balaton offensive, begun on 6 and 7 March, was reported to Hitler. Forgetting that he himself had ordered the offensive, he indulged in one of his much-feared fits of frenetic rage. In his opinion the only reason for the failure of this attack was a lack of the proverbial fanatic dedication on the part of the commander of the Southern Army Group, General Wöhler. With fists clenched he shouted at Guderian: 'Wöhler has always taken a negative and arrogant attitude towards National Socialism. He is incapable of inspiration. How could I expect a man like that to stand up to such gruelling ordeals?'

Wöhler was dismissed at once.

Another example of the Führer's victimization was Colonel von Bonin. His downfall followed the collapse of the German Vistula Front after the start of the Russian offensive on the 12, 13, and 14 January 1945. At this juncture Hitler had issued the famous 'fortress' order, according to which 'fortresses' had to be held and defended in all circumstances 'to the last man and to the last drop of blood'. The term 'fortresses' did not mean, as one might suppose, fortified towns or sites which boasted armoured fortress works, supply depots, artillery strength and large garrisons, and which were therefore particularly well placed to resist enemy attacks over a long period. It referred instead to unfortified towns or localities which were designated as fortresses by

Hitler before or even during an attack, on account of their position in the traffic network or for some other reason. With a very few exceptions, they had nothing whatsoever in common with the traditional concept of a fortress other than Hitler's demand that they be used for this purpose.

Warsaw was one of these places which were supposed to be defended to the last man. Five thousand men were stationed there under the command of a general. The fortress order reached the commanding officer in Warsaw twelve hours too late. Thus it came about that the German garrison withdrew on 16 and 17 January 1945. Hitler blamed Bonin, at that time Chief of Operational Staff, Army High Command, for the late arrival of the order, and although he had no proof that it was his fault, he handed him and his two assistants over to the Gestapo. Bonin disappeared into the prison near the Lehrter railway station in Berlin, and thence into a concentration camp. Later, when the subject of the appointment of a fortress commandant at Frankfurt an der Oder was under discussion, Jodl said to Hitler: 'If you want the best and ablest officer for the defence of the fortress at Frankfurt, Führer, there is only one possible choice. I refer, of course, to Colonel von Bonin.'

Hitler flared up immediately. 'Any man who can't carry out my orders promptly,' he bristled, 'is of no use to me!' That was the end of the matter, and Colonel von Bonin remained in the concentration camp until the end of the war.

Hitler's uncontrollable rage was even worse when he was informed of the defeat or – as he saw it – the failure of a dedicated Nazi: he never took the trouble to check the accuracy of his information or investigate the causes of the defeat. On 14 April 1945 Hitler was told of the fall of Vienna. The Sixth SS *Panzer* Army, led by SS Lieutenant General Sepp Dietrich, had fought in Austria in the area around Vienna.

This Nazi 'old warrior' had been the leader of the '*Leibstandarte* Adolf Hitler' (Hitler's personal SS regiment) before 1933. These divisions were amongst the toughest and most battle-tried left in the German Army at this point. Yet when Hitler heard of the retreat of the Sixth SS *Panzer* Army and the fall of Vienna, he raved like a madman and sent the following radio message to Dietrich: 'The Führer is of the opinion that the troops did not fight as the situation demanded and orders that the SS divisions "Adolf Hitler", "*Das Reich*", "Skull" and "*Hohenstaufen*" be stripped of their arm-bands.'

The arm-bands on the forearm of their uniforms had the same symbolic meaning, or at least they were supposed to, as the traditional badges of the 'Old Army'. On receiving the message from Hitler Dietrich radioed back that he would sooner shoot himself than obey this order.

In February and March 1945 developments in the west were as catastrophic as in the east. The American and British armies flooded farther and farther into Germany, crossing the Rhine first at Remagen, and swiftly establishing other bridgeheads across the river. There was hardly a pause in their advance. At this point Hitler, supported by Goebbel's propaganda machine, proclaimed the adoption of the fighting methods and organization called 'Werewolf', that is, fighting by ambush. Modelled mainly on the Russian and Polish partisans, this equivalent of the underground movements in formerly German-occupied countries was to be created overnight out of thin air. Children, women, girls and old men, all were to be involved, all were to destroy the enemy in hit-and-run strikes.

Did Hitler really imagine that this desperate enterprise could produce any military success or in any way delay the overall outcome of the war? Did he really think that the German people would follow him into annihilation? Or did he see himself as the principal figure in a huge, horrifically realistic Wagner opera, standing in the midst of the flames? Did he want to drag the whole nation with him into the 'twilight of the gods' of his 'thousand-year Reich'? It is difficult to say what went on in his mind. Hitler had long since lost contact with the people, he no longer knew them. The people were sick of war, totally exhausted and bled dry after almost six years of it, with all the terrors of bombing. They wanted peace, nothing but peace. The Werewolf group, even if it was to achieve only a modicum of success, would have had to be prepared well in advance. In Russia and in the Ukraine, partisan warfare had been a success because, among other reasons, the fronts were far too long and Germany did not have enough troops to man these huge areas. In France, Norway and Denmark it had succeeded because the underground movements in these countries were supported with weapons and propaganda by the Allies and because these nations could rely on assistance from abroad in the near future. In Germany none of these things were true.

It very soon became clear that the newly formed Werewolf group was completely ineffectual against the rapid advance of the Allied armies. By then even Hitler's élite troops no longer responded to his appeals. When the Sixth SS Mountain Division, which had been brought in from Norway, was surrounded by American troops in the Taunus mountains, Hitler gave this five-thousand strong division the order to split up into small parties and join the Werewolf organization. But they failed to respond to this call.

Whilst the Werewolf operation in the west was supposed to play at the very least a delaying role, a propaganda and press campaign was launched in eastern Germany to incite the civilian population to the most extreme resistance against the Red Army. In the middle of March 1945 even Guderian was drawn into this press campaign. By this time the terrible, endless stream of despairing refugees from the east had grown to a torrent. On both sides of the major roads from the east there had arisen a wall of broken-down vehicles, people and animals starved or frozen to death. Train after train rolled into the stations in Berlin with refugees from the east, many of whom had been snowed under in open cattle wagons and had died of frostbite. During these weeks death reaped all too great a harvest. Everywhere there was unspeakable misery and horrifying distress.

But Adolf Hitler saw nothing of all this, or did not want to see it, for fear of impairing his 'inspiration'. During the last years of the war he rarely left his headquarters near Rastenburg in East Prussia, which were set amongst magnificent grazing lands, great forests and lakes. This peace and beauty was in strange contrast to the terrors of the war. But for Hitler the war consisted only of figures, of blue and red lines on the General Staff maps. He never once arranged to be shown films of the actual destruction caused by bombing, which might have given him at least a vague picture of the reality. What could Hitler possibly know about the sufferings of the civilian population? His closest associates in the Party and in government took great pains, in fact, to keep everything unpleasant from him, so as not to disturb this fatal self-deception, although it is impossible to say whether they did so out of weakness of character, cowardice and fear of Hitler, or insufficient courage in recognizing the truth about themselves. Hitler had once called Churchill a 'military idiot', but whilst Churchill was clambering over the rubble of London and inspiring the people with fresh courage, even visiting his soldiers close behind the front lines, smoking his cigar and armed with a walking stick, Adolf Hitler crawled off to hide in the forests of East Prussia behind barricades of heavily-armed sentries and did not appear at the front or amongst the civilian population in the bomb-ravaged cities. Only once did Hitler cast a quick glance over the destruction in Berlin. That was in November 1944, when he left his headquarters at 'Wolf's Lair' near Rastenburg and travelled, via Berlin, to the neighbourhood of Bad Nauheim. As he passed through the suburbs of Berlin in his special train, he was appalled by the sight of the devastation. He had not had the slightest idea, so he remarked to those around him, that the effects of bombing were so devastating. Yet on the other hand he found enough time to busy himself with the most trivial things. Matters of state and military decisions affecting the life and death of thousands had to wait when there was a new medal to be designed. As late as March 1945 he arranged that sketches for a new medal be brought from the factories for his inspection. He could spend hours too on his fantastic plans for the reconstruction of Berlin and other German cities. It may be objected that this represented recreation and relaxation for him, that Roosevelt too had his stamp collection, but the 'idiots' Churchill and Roosevelt at least had enough sense to leave military business to their generals.

Hitler saw himself as both supreme statesman and supreme military commander. But he would allow no one else to try to combine politics with fighting. In spite of this, when early in 1945 the economic, as well as the military situation, began to drift hopelessly, Guderian felt himself compelled to intervene. On the evening of 23 January, the envoy Dr Barandon had arrived to present himself to Guderian in his capacity as the new liaison officer between the Reich Foreign Ministry and the Chief of the General Staff. On his first visit Barandon received from Guderian such a revealing and candid account of the causes and the scope of the collapse of the German eastern front since 12 January 1945 that probably the only parallel he could find for the military situation at that time was the collapse of the front in October 1918. The climax of Guderian's remarks was a demand to the Foreign Office for immediate armistice negotiations with our adversaries in the west.

During the night Barandon conveyed the inescapable conclusions of this interview to the Reich Foreign Ministry. But such nocturnal negotiations met with no response and ended fruitlessly. In the Foreign Office they were not prepared to ask Hitler for a decision on the possibility of an armistice, let alone unconditional capitulation to the Western powers. Two days later Guderian most urgently repeated his appeal to the Foreign Office for immediate armistice negotiations in the west, but this time without an intermediary. These exchanges took place on 25 January. Once again there was no result.

The negotiations between Guderian and the Foreign Office came to Hitler's attention on that same day through a note from ambassador Walter Hewel, the permanent representative of the Foreign Office at the Führer's headquarters. At the conference held on the same evening Hitler referred trenchantly to his 'Basic Order No. 1', which he had issued in 1939, at the beginning of the war. In this order it was laid down that nobody was entitled to pass information from his own sphere of duty to other departments. Hitler reinforced his remarks with the words: 'So if the Chief of the General Staff informs the Foreign Office about the military situation in the east, with the intention of securing their intervention in favour of an armistice, he is thereby committing treason.'

Later Guderian tried several times to intervene politically, aiming for an immediate armistice in the west. In the middle

The author, Gerhard Boldt, captain in the 13th Cavalry Regiment

Reinhard Gelen's staff in 1944

The author and his men on campaign

Gehlen in coversation with colleagues in January 1945. On his right is his eventual successor, Lieutenant Wessel

Hitler in Poland visiting the Eastern Front, March 1945

A map-reading session at the Führer's headquarters: from the left—Göring, von Below, (standing), Hitler, Keitel

General Guderian

Hitler with
Bormann

1945: Lancasters of RAF Bomber Command on a raid over Germany

The Reich Chancellery in Berlin

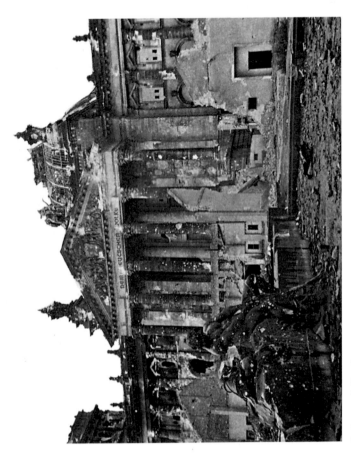

before and after the war

A mother searching for her child among a heap of children's corpses

The wreckage of the Reich Chancellery immediately after the war

Hitler viewing bomb damage in Berlin

Hitler surrounded by children at a rally. In the background stands Baldur von Schirach, leader of the Youth Movement

Hitler with the son of one of Eva Braun's friends

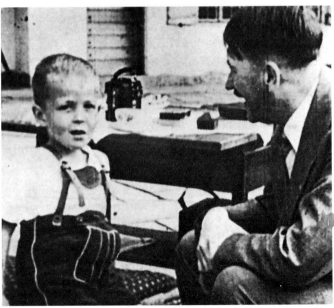

Casualties of the
Allied air attacks

In the Reich
Chancellery
gardens in March
1945. From the
left: Axmann,
Fegelein, Schaub,
Hitler, General
Burgdorff, Linge

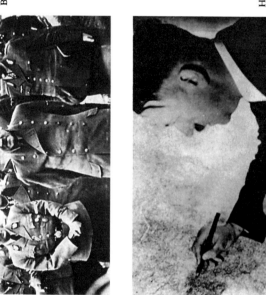

Hitler at his eastern
headquarters
studying a map of
the Russian Front

Two of the last photographs of Hitler.

He is awarding the Iron Cross to members of the Hitler Youth, who had fought bravely in Germany's defence.

This family was lucky to escape alive

The final battle
for Berlin

Allied units advance
through Germany

The defeat

**Men of the 71st
Regiment of the
7th Army mopping
up resistance from
street fighters**

Russian women soldiers in Berlin

In the Chancellery garden an American soldier is looking in the hastily dug trench for the half-burnt bodies of Hitler and Eva Braun

July 1945. A Russian officer and an American captain (standing) at the remains of Hitler's great marble table in the Chancery

The great Nazi eagle from the Chancellery among the debris

of March 1945 he learned from neutral radio stations about certain peace soundings taken by a Dr Hesse in Stockholm. Once again the envoy Dr Barandon acted as intermediary between Guderian and the Foreign Office. But these conversations in the Wilhelmstrasse, to which I accompanied the Colonel-General, ended like the rest without any positive result.

Guderian and Barandon realized that there was no sense in making efforts to obtain an armistice through the Foreign Office. It was probably not the right approach in wartime. Moreover, in the course of the war the diplomats had increasingly lost their influence on Hitler and had been largely discredited in his eyes. (This development, taken to its logical conclusion, found expression in Hitler's Political Testament.)

Guderian therefore resolved to make further efforts towards the same end through Himmler and Göring. On the day after the second interview in the Foreign Office Guderian went to the headquarters of the Army Group Vistula at Prenzlau to see Himmler, its commander, and to try to persuade him to resign his post. Himmler resigned, without raising any objections. He was probably quite glad to make this decision anyway. One reason for his readiness to oblige may have been a certain recognition of the truth about himself, another may also have been the fact that by resigning he was regaining his old freedom of movement. (His successor was Colonel-General Heinrici, who until this juncture had led an Army Group in Slovakia.) At this meeting in Prenzlau Guderian also discussed with Himmler the necessity of immediate armistice negotiations. Shortly afterwards, on 21 March, the two of them met in the Reich Chancellery, and Guderian harangued Himmler once again on the same subject, with great urgency. Himmler appeared receptive and interested, but refused to give Guderian any support whatsoever, believing that Hitler would have him shot if he were even to approach him with proposals of that kind, let alone demand anything.

Once again, Hitler heard of this conversation on the same day, and at the conference that evening, 21 March, he urged Guderian, in a way which left no room for misunderstanding, to take a cure at a spa because of his 'heart complaint'. Guderian did not, however, comply at once with Hitler's 'wish', because the man named as his successor, General Krebs, was not yet completely recovered from a head injury.

Working against time, Guderian and Barandon hastily decided to approach Göring with their plan. Himmler, who was let in on the secret, offered to speak to Göring himself. At Karinhall, Göring's private palace, the two of them had a discussion lasting some four hours. Göring too was persuaded of the necessity for immediate armistice negotiations, but like the others he refused to approach Hitler. He too was firmly convinced that Hitler would throw him out or even have him locked up. Thus Guderian's endeavours to bring the war to a speedy end, or at least the war against the Western Allies, ended in failure, in spite of his dedication and disregard of personal risk. At the same time his involvement on the military side was also drawing to a close.

Pushing past Küstrin on both sides, the Russians, in the course of their winter offensive, had formed a small bridge-head on the west bank of the Oder, to the west of Küstrin. By smaller operations during February and March they continually enlarged this bridgehead, which presented the gravest threat to Berlin. On 10 March Kietz, a suburb of Küstrin, was lost. On 13 March Küstrin, which had previously been declared a 'fortress' by Hitler, was surrounded by the Russians. SS Lieutenant-General Reinefarth was appointed by Hitler as fortress commandant of Küstrin.

Under pressure from headquarters, on 23 and 24 March the Ninth Army under General Busse made the first attempt to crush the bridgehead or at least to restore links with Küstrin. For this venture General Busse had at his disposal the Twentieth and Twenty-Fifth *Panzer* Grenadier Divisions. Since the Soviets had understandably organized huge concentrations of troops and above all artillery in the Küstrin bridgehead, and our forces with their two divisions were far too weak, nothing was achieved. Our own losses were very high, due especially to the enemy artillery.

Guderian now stepped in and added two further divisions to the Ninth Army for a repetition of the attack. On 27 March the assault on the Küstrin bridgehead, carried out by the Twentieth and Twenty-fifth *Panzer* Grenadier divisions, the 'Führer-escort' division and the 'Müncheberg' division, achieved by dint of surprise an initial advance to a depth of about three kilometres. Then the attack was halted, with heavy losses on our side. It had proved impossible to eliminate the bridgehead or to restore our links with Küstrin. About lunchtime on 27 March the commander of the Vistula Army Group, Colonel-General Heinrici, reported the failure of the attack on Küstrin to Guderian. I well remember how dejected Guderian was when he received the news. He had firmly believed that we might achieve at least a partial success. The men had fought well, but they had been overwhelmingly outnumbered. It was in this spirit that Guderian reported the failure to Hitler on the same afternoon at the situation conference in the Reich Chancellery. At this news, Hitler completely lost control of himself and launched into wild abuse of General Busse, the leader of the Ninth Army, in whose area the Küstrin bridgehead lay. Hitler's attitude was totally unfair; his recriminations against Busse and the troops lacked any sense of reality whatsoever. At the conclusion of this stormy interview he requested Guderian to report to him with General Busse on 28 March at 2 pm, to give an account of the battle. On the same day, late on 27 March, Guderian delivered a letter to Hitler, in which he reported on the operation at Küstrin and the preparations for it. In clear and objective fashion he set out the proportionate strength of the German assault units to the defending Soviet forces and the catastrophic level of our own losses. In the concluding sentence of his letter he rejected in unusually sharp terms the grave charges which Hitler had made against General Busse that afternoon.

On 28 March Guderian and Busse appeared in the Reich Chancellery at the time fixed by Hitler. After an impersonal and frosty greeting Busse was made to start at once on his report on the assault operation at Küstrin. But he had not even got beyond the introductory sentences when Hitler engulfed him in a torrent of purely personal abuse. His angry reproaches were directed not only at Busse, but also at the troops who had carried out the attack. Then Guderian's loud, forceful voice burst into Hitler's flood of words and cut him short in mid-sentence. In spite of his agitation he clearly and unambiguously hurled at Hitler the arguments he had used the evening before, word for word. He rejected in their entirety Hitler's recriminations about the planning, the leadership and the troops. Hitler could not get another word in. He slumped farther and farther down in his chair, all the colour draining from his face.

But then, suddenly, he got up from his armchair with an agility which nobody present would have thought possible. His face was marked by large red blotches. His left arm, the whole left-hand side of his body, was trembling more violently than usual, and it looked as if he was about to throw himself at Guderian and attack him physically. Guderian stood rooted to the spot like the rest of those present. For some seconds it was so quiet that the agitated breathing of the two men could be clearly heard. Then Hitler poured out a stream of invective, accusation and loathing. The subject was no longer Küstrin and the battles on the Oder. The torrent of words was now directed not only at Guderian, but at the whole of the General Staff, at the whole Officer Corps. Hitler laid the blame for every failure in the last few months at their door. Here again, in its most extreme form, the gulf between the old Officer Corps and the Party was revealed. Two different worlds were confronting each other. Guderian, in his turn, became more and more vehement. He repeated all his old demands and his criticisms of Hitler's military leadership: the hopeless offensive in the Ardennes, the surrender of the Curland Front and the delayed withdrawal of the twenty-three divisions, the need for a ruthless weakening of the western front in favour of the eastern front, the troop concentrations required for the Lake Balaton offensive and Hitler's unscrupulous abandonment of the population of eastern Germany.

Then at last the bystanders awoke from the numbed inactivity into which they had been plunged by this unique and extraordinary exchange. Major von Freytag-Loringhoven, General Guderian's assistant, was afraid that Guderian would be arrested at any moment. He hurried to the telephone in the ante-room, rang General Krebs and, having described the situation in the Reich Chancellery to him and explained his fears, begged him to tie Guderian up on the telephone with important messages from the front.

In the meantime General Thomale and one of the officers present had tried to separate Guderian from Hitler, whilst one of Hitler's adjutants was literally pushing him cautiously back into his armchair. Guderian went into the ante-room and spoke to Krebs. When he returned to the conference room self-control had reasserted itself over the scene, although nothing at all had happened in between. Hitler put a few more trivial questions to General Busse and then closed the subject of the Küstrin bridgehead. Then followed the usual conference. The atmosphere in the room was intolerably tense and oppressive. The individual speeches were very short and terse. Scarcely any questions were asked. Everybody was desperate to get away from the Chancellery as quickly as possible.

At the end of the conference Hitler asked Keitel and Guderian to stay behind. Guderian was relieved of his post and sent on leave. Two days later, on 30 March, Guderian left the German headquarters in Zossen for good, having first handed over to his successor, General Krebs.

As soon as Guderian was requested by Hitler to quit his post and the headquarters, Major von Freytag-Loringhoven asked for an immediate transfer and a posting to a division at the front. But Guderian's successor, General Krebs, managed very skilfully to induce von Freytag-Loringhoven to stick somewhat reluctantly to his post of adjutant to the Chief of General Staff.

I myself was kept on by General Krebs as ADC to the Chief of General Staff and had to accompany him very frequently to the conferences in the Reich Chancellery.

Two days after Guderian's dismissal, on 30 March, I accompanied General Krebs to a conference. The report on the eastern front, which Krebs gave, centred on the break-out from the 'fortress' Küstrin of around one thousand men under the command of SS Lieutenant-General Reinefarth, which had not been authorized by Hitler. Hitler accepted this news almost without protest, which was all the more incomprehensible – although it once again clearly demonstrated his incalculable moods – since it was only two days previously that he and Guderian had had that remarkable argument, in which Küstrin had played a not inconsiderable role.

General Heinrici had been ordered to give a report to Hitler on that day. Heinrici was Supreme Commander of Army Group Vistula, including the Third Tank Army and the Ninth Army, those troops in fact who had to defend the front protecting Berlin against the expected Russian attack. It was the first time that the General and Hitler had met. Outwardly Heinrici appeared restrained and modest, but he made up for it by being all the more firm and intransigent, obdurate even, in defending his point of view. Heinrici's main aim in his exposition of the current situation of his Army Group was to prevail upon Hitler to relieve Frankfurt an der Oder of its fortress status. Heinrici hoped thus to release two divisions which he urgently needed to bolster up the far too thinly defended Oder front. Hitler listened to Heinrici's well-founded arguments perfectly quietly and asked Krebs for some papers in connection with the area of Frankfurt an der Oder. I quickly found the relevant documents from amongst the mass of material which I brought with me, and I handed them to Hitler, who studied them in silence. (Although Hitler wore glasses, papers intended for him had to be typed on a typewriter manufactured especially for him with an extra large typeface.)

Then, quite without warning, Hitler raised himself on the arms of his chair, got up and began loudly and hysterically to quote the key sentences of his well-known fortress order, going on then to deal with the 'fortress' of Frankfurt an der Oder. He abused Heinrici, the General Staff, the generals and the officers as a body, claiming that they had never understood or wanted to understand his fortress order for reasons of cowardice and lack of determination. As abruptly as this outburst had begun, so too it was suddenly all over, and Hitler sank back into his chair completely exhausted. Even today I can still see Heinrici's stupefied face. Thunderstruck, he looked questioningly from one bystander to another. But none of the military leaders, chosen as they were by Hitler and constantly in his presence, were prepared to take Heinrici's part against the Führer. Heinrici went on obstinately fighting for his point of view, completely unsupported. Later on in the course of the discussion the question of the fortress commandant for Frankfurt an der Oder came up again. Hitler wanted a *Gneisenau*, harking back to the history of the Napoleonic Wars in Germany. Heinrici wanted Colonel Bieler, because he considered him a sound, conscientious officer experienced in combat. When it emerged in the next few days that Hitler did not want Colonel Bieler as fortress commandant, despite Heinrici's keenness to appoint him, and that neither of the two military command staffs was supporting Heinrici's cause, the General offered his resignation. Thereupon Hitler gave way and agreed, without any new motivating factors at all, to Heinrici's wishes.

Some of the most powerful men in Hitler's circle were those least well known to the public. Much has already been written about Himmler and Goebbels but little more is known about *Reichsleiter* Martin Bormann than that he was one of the most strongly anti-clerical and anti-Christian men in the NSDAP (Nazi Party).

Martin Bormann worked as an agricultural administrator before he was taken into the Party leadership. After the seizure of power, he worked with Hess in the Central Filing Office until 1939, after which he became his *Stabsleiter* and, at the beginning of the war, link-man between the NSDAP under

Hess, and Hitler. From this point on, he worked tirelessly to consolidate his own position of power. The first task he set himself was to eradicate Hess's influence on Hitler as completely and quickly as possible. He mastered the art of gradually distancing Hess from Hitler and, in the course of time, alienated the two men completely from each other. There is no doubt that Bormann was an outstanding judge of human nature. He very quickly recognized Hitler's weaknesses and learnt how to make use of them to his own advantage. By small personal attentions he wormed his way into Hitler's confidence. He had the knack of taking up Hitler's ideas and thoughts and drafting them into well-formulated orders which he then promptly submitted to Hitler for his signature. The Führer was most favourably impressed by these attentions, which bolstered his self-esteem. Thus it was that in April 1943 Bormann was officially appointed the Führer's Secretary.

Another trick of Bormann's was to encourage Hitler's obsessive belief that he was infallible and therefore God-like, by exaggerated displays of hero-worship. After Hess had flown to Scotland on 10 May 1941, Bormann had the field to himself. From then on, he proceeded to establish himself as Hitler's immediate confidant and adviser. Although as *Reichsleiter* he presided only over the Party Chancellery, he wasted no time in getting himself appointed to the other three: the Reich Chancellery, the Presidential Chancellery and the Chancellery of the Führer of the NSDAP. Anyone who wanted access to Hitler or had anything to submit to him could approach him only through Bormann. This was true not merely of Party matters but also for important state affairs. Everything passed through his hands before Hitler saw it. His personal ambition led to the banishment of all those who refused to take orders from him. It is likely that

Bormann intended some day to seize supreme power for himself: it would certainly have been the logical conclusion to his ambitious climb. He was hated by all those who worked close to him. His manner is well illustrated by a brief marginal note which he once wrote on a document belonging to a higher ranking SS leader: 'I do not consort with idiots.' Bormann did not have a single friend among Hitler's associates: he was feared – and respected – by everyone.

The *Gauleiter* Koch, who also had frequent entrée to Hitler, was very like Bormann in some ways. He was heavier and more uncouth and his facial features were even more coarse and brutal, but he was Bormann's equal in ambition, egoism and arrogance. The following story about him is typical: during the war, while he was visiting Göring's magnificent residence, Karinhall, Koch had boasted to Göring that for the autumn hunting season, which was only a few months away, he would build a much more beautiful hunting residence. Consequently, in the middle of the war, while Allied Air Forces were reducing one German town after another to heaps of rubble, this *Gauleiter* had his castle, Buchenhofn, near Zichenau, altered into a pleasure-seat at a cost of several million marks. Because German 'marble' was not beautiful enough for him, he used valuable foreign currency to import Swedish marble. Nor, when the troops flowing back from the east passed near Zichenau, would Koch allow his castle to be turned into a hospital for badly-wounded German soldiers. One estate after another passed into his private possession. When he became Reich Kommissar for the Ukraine, he got Hitler to appoint him to the Bialystock district as well so that he could say his rule extended from the Baltic to the Black Sea.

After the capture of Königsberg in April 1945, the encircled Third and Fourth Army in East Prussia carried on their desperate but hopeless struggle whilst hundreds and thousands of East Prussian refugees waited for transport to take them to the west. Koch was apparently quite unmoved by the appalling situation in his territory. He took part in conferences at the Reich Chancellery as if nothing had happened. Interestingly enough, in April 1945 Koch made a bid to escape from the Reich Chancellery with its dangerous proximity to Hitler, and to reach safety. He merely exchanged his Party uniform for a windcheater, probably because he had good reason to fear that the people of Berlin would have killed him had they recognized him. Hitler did not hang Koch as he did thousands of soldiers and officers who attempted to escape with their life from some hopeless trap. He was simply never seen again.

Another typical representative of the inner guard of the Party was *Reichshauptamtsleiter* Saur. It was he, together with Speer, who was responsible for the overall arms and munitions production. An unscrupulous intriguer and swindler, his ox-like physique alone would have qualified him for the select group whose blind obedience and total lack of scruples seemed to endear them to Hitler. Saur, too, had an insatiable lust for power. Characteristic of the man is the following occurrence which I myself witnessed. In the course of the heavy fighting in Hungary in March 1945, the Army Group South urgently needed a fresh supply of small arms. At the same time, a large armaments factory in Central Slovakia was under threat from the Red Army which had drawn dangerously close. There were some twenty thousand guns still in this factory. When Hitler heard this, he duly passed the information on to Speer, directing him to have these guns supplied to Army Group South without delay. When Speer did not immediately agree to this, Hitler sent for Speer's deputy, Saur. Saur clicked his heels together, jerked up his arm and greeted Hitler with flashing eyes and a loud 'Heil, my Führer!' This was Hitler's man. When Hitler put the situation to him, he agreed enthusiastically and volunteered to supply the guns to the troops within forty-eight hours. That was the end of the matter and Hitler was quite satisfied. Not so, however, the troops, who never actually received the guns because they never left the factory. It was after this that in Hitler's will and testament Saur was appointed Speer's successor.

4. THE DISPERSAL OF GERMAN HEADQUARTERS

On 15 April, the Ninth Army was again subjected to heavy attacks to the east of Berlin. The Russian troop concentrations, particularly of artillery, on both sides of the Küstrin–Berlin highway were exceptionally strong here. The Russian Air Force, too, was significantly more active than on the preceding days, particularly in flights over the front-line area. Along the whole front lay a tension which was close to breaking-point. From all my own years at the front I know this awful tension only too well. A soldier lying in the middle of it all is obsessed by an irrepressible urge to scream.

The Party and State heads, however, preferred to ignore all this. Everything, the wireless, all the newspapers, propaganda proclamations, the conferences and talks between the leaders, almost all revolved, like a roundabout, around one theme only, the death of the US President on 12 April. Although there was no reason whatsoever to believe that this event would make any difference to the political situation, Goebbels, Minister for Propaganda, declared the death of Roosevelt to be a miracle, even a turning-point in Germany's destiny. Once again, Goebbels rolled out his entire repertoire of impassioned rhetoric. He compared Roosevelt's death with that of the Tsarina Elisabeth in the last year of the Seven Years War which saved Prussia from certain defeat. He bombarded the people with words to convince them that the American-Soviet Alliance was on the point of breaking up and that the war must now end in victory for Germany.

Then came 16 April and, for the soldiers at the front, the final snapping of this oppressive tension: for that day revealed to the Germans behind the front line and in Berlin the hollowness of Goebbels's propaganda-myth about Roosevelt's death.

While darkness still lay over everything, the Russians, using several thousand guns, began an intense bombardment of the Ninth Army and the Fourth Tank Army in the Lausitz. The scene was indescribable. When this unbelievable concentration of artillery fire started up it was as if the curtain had gone up on the final act of the last great battle of this world. Miles of Russian batteries stood drawn up in close formation, literally touching one another. The bombardment lasted for hours. Then the Russian regiments, divisions and armies launched their attack. In the Lausitz, where the Fourth Tank Army was lying between Muskau and Forst, the attack began at 7.30 am, and where the Ninth Army was stationed on the Oder, at 6.30 am.

It was only in the orders of the day which Hitler sent out to the soldiers on the eastern front on this 16 April that the death of Roosevelt was mentioned again. Once again he promised them that Roosevelt's death would change the course of destiny in their favour, promising them: 'Berlin will stay German; Vienna will be restored to Germans.' Meanwhile, in the streets of Berlin, feverish activity had begun. The distant dull booming which as yet hardly sounded like the thunder of real artillery drove the inhabitants out of their houses or cellars in the early hours. The last batch of newly-recruited *Volkssturm* men hurried to the collecting points: by midday the first detachments were on their way by local train to their assembly areas behind the front. Anti-tank obstacles were set up in and around Berlin leaving only narrow access points. Women and girls stood around in huddled groups, listening in dread to the distant sounds from the front. Would the Red Army capture their city or would it be possible to hold them up until the Americans, who were already in Zerbst, east of the Elbe, reached Berlin? The same questions were repeated over and over again on the tired, careworn faces of the people hurrying along the streets or forming queues outside food shops. This panic-ridden fear which one saw everywhere was the result of propaganda about the atrocities perpetrated by the Red Army. One hope alone kept them from panicking, the hope that the Americans would come. They must come, they must . . .

I was sitting in the ante-room to the office of the Chief of the Army General Staff, General Krebs, at the headquarters in Zossen. One frantic telephone call followed another. Frequently all three telephones on my desk were in use at once. The General rang and I entered his room by the sound-proof double door. He was standing at the big table, bending over maps marked in red and blue to indicate the line of the Oder Front. I had to remind him that I was there. Only then did he stand up. The small plump general who was generally so jovial gazed at me with tired eyes: 'I wanted to ask you to put me through to General Burgdorf again – I want to find out once and for all where we are meant to be transferring Headquarters; try and get through to Berchtesgaden, and send Freytag in to me; oh, and bring me another glass of vermouth please.' I returned to my room and put in the calls to Berchtesgaden and the Reich Chancellery. Then I went to find Adjutant von Freytag-Loringhoven. It was he who had told me that morning, shortly after Reveille, that Russian artillery fire had commenced around Küstrin at 3.50 am and that three hours later the Russians had attacked. It was now nearly 10 am. Reports from the front had been less frequent in the last hour, the telephone wires having no doubt been brought down by artillery fire.

Involuntarily I found myself thinking of my comrades out there. By this time the battle must have reached its climax. How often had I myself stood there in the thick of it, had I, like the men lying out there now in the hell of battle, dug my hands into the protective earth, somewhere in the vast expanse of the Russian countryside. Only soldiers know what it feels like to be lying badly wounded somewhere in the middle of a battle like that, and the feeling of relief when comrades come and drag one out of the muddy, shell-pitted ground to safety. All the young men at headquarters longed to be out there, taking part in the fighting. This impotent waiting, knowing that the struggle was hopeless was so hard to bear. No one who has not feared for the safety of his country can understand what it was like.

The Major and I stood silent for a few minutes and listened, each sunk in his own thoughts, each doubtless thinking the same thing. He, the once smart officer who never showed personal feelings, looked tired now; we had worked for so long day in, day out and through the nights as well. He looked wordlessly at me, stood up and went in to the general. I got the vermouth out of the safe and poured out a glass. Shortly afterwards, following a brief air-raid warning, five Russian fighters roared overhead, a new experience for us since up to now the Russian Air Force had seldom ventured farther than twenty kilometres into enemy territory unless they were certain they would not encounter any German fighter planes. The telephones rang endlessly: it was always the same question: 'Any news from the front?'

Just before 11 am, my room filled with generals and colonels: at 11 there was to be a briefing conference with the Chief of the Army General Staff. That day the discussion in my ante-room was livelier than usual: 'Where are we to evacuate to? What preparations are we to make?' These and similar questions buzzed through the room. It was still just possible to get back to Berchtesgaden through Bohemia but how long would that be true? The telephone conversation between Burgdorf and Krebs had not clarified the situation. Hitler had still not decided where the Führer Headquarters and all its ancillary staff should go. While the conference was going on, I was asked to take a call from a sergeant in our advance party, who had got back to Berchtesgaden a few days before by special train. General Kreb's wife and daughter had gone with him, so I inquired about all the things the General wanted to know. And then the voice at the other end asked me: 'What's going to happen to us?' How could I tell? There was not a soul in Germany who had the faintest idea what was going to happen next.

At midday the first detailed report from the front came in: 'The attack has been repulsed, fighting for some positions is still going on. Losses are very high.' It was the same old formula again, the one we had heard at Leningrad, on the Volchov, on the Ilmensee, in the Pripiet marshes, in front of Warsaw. . . . That afternoon, punctually at 4 pm, the Russian artillery fire began again: it went on, as before, for an hour and a half and then as before, they attacked, wave after wave of them. By evening incoming reports announced: 'The front is still holding, deeper enemy incursions have been contained. Send us soldiers, send us ammunition.'

The Russians pushed our front back a few kilometres in several places both south and north of Frankfurt. At the bridgehead west of Küstrin Russian troops had made a deeper incursion on both sides of the Küstrin–Berlin highway and advanced as far as the altitude line on the edge of the Oder plain. They had also made another breakthrough.

Towards 10 pm, Krebs and the Major, who had gone with

him that day, returned from the conference in the Reich Chancellery. I had already given instructions for a snack to be put out on their desks so that they could have a quick meal before their real work began: I knew it would probably go on until 3 or 4 am, if not all night. The Major reported over a cup of coffee:

'They will have to abandon the position west of Küstrin tonight. The main combat line is being set back to the Hardenberg position. It's almost all over up there in front: they may just be able to hold the Hardenberg position for another twenty-four hours. He said that the situation in the west was just as bad, and in the north, the English are advancing on Lüneburg. The Americans have crossed the Elbe between Magdeburg and Dessau. They are closer to Berlin than the Russians, in Saxony they are pressing Halle and Leipzig and in the south, they have entered Bavaria. The Russians are lying in front of Brünn and west of Vienna. In the Lausitz between Muskau and Forst the first day of the Russian attack on the Fourth Tank Army, like that on the Ninth, had achieved the first enemy incursions and although these have been contained, it is hardly likely that the front line can resist further heavy attack. Our own forces are too weak and there are hardly any reserves.'

He paused and gazed ahead of him, probably thinking of his wife and child who lived near Leipzig. 'Another thing,' he continued, 'when we were driving through Tempelhof this evening, a group of people yelled at us, "Vampires! That's what you are, vampires!" ' He went back to his desk and looked through his post.

Next day, 17 April, the battles outside Berlin and in the Lausitz continued with undiminished violence. The Russian attack forced back the German divisions step by step. This time the evening report from the Fourth Tank Army read: 'Our own lines maintained their position in general. The Air Force lent support, making 1,000 sorties.' Thanks to a counter-attack by the *Kurmark* division on the Küstrin–Berlin highway, the Ninth Army had managed to halt the Russian attack. Fighting was still going on around the other incursion points. The corps on the left wing of the Ninth Army again repulsed the enemy attack and maintained the front line.

18 April brought glorious spring weather and with it renewed heavy fighting. The Russian attack thrust deeper into the south. Bitter fighting broke out in Silesia and in the woodland areas of the Lausitz where the superior strength of the Soviet Army was particularly telling. Towards 9 am, one of our newsmen managed to get a call through to my wife in Lübeck. Although she did not know how desperate the situation really was, she was full of anxious queries: 'Everyone is saying that the Russians are outside Berlin. I'm so afraid for you – can you still hear me? Can't you get back here? What is going to happen? Is it true what people are saying, that the English are outside Lüneburg?' I could not reply to all these questions, because we were cut off. That was our last conversation, and barely four weeks later she was told that I had died in Berlin.

It was on 19 April that the first serious Russian breakthroughs occurred. In the early hours of the morning, the Russian tank spearheads from the main battle area around Muskau–Forst–Guben reached the Bautzen area. At Spremberg the Russians crossed the Spree. We lost Forst. This Russian offensive was aiming as the General Staff had foreseen at the rear of Berlin, and not at Prague, as Hitler had said it would. Our units in the area between Forst and Fürstenberg were also pushed back sharply. In the area east of Berlin where fighting was going on, the Russians were advancing on Jahnsfeld and Müncheberg and they succeeded in taking Wriezen ... North of Buckow, 150 enemy tanks broke through. It was only outside Frankfurt itself that units of the Ninth Army were able to retain their position on the Oder. By evening on the nineteenth, it was clear from the direction of the main Russian offensives that they were trying to encircle Berlin and the Ninth Army from the north and from the south. That day Goebbels read over the radio a proclamation to the German people, which appeared the next day, Hitler's birthday, in all the newspapers which were still being published. It repeated the promise Hitler had given to the troops: 'Berlin will stay German, Vienna will be restored to Germany.' Even now many Germans still believed Hitler's promises. They had been lied to so often, trained to believe Goebbels' propaganda. They still believed in the famous secret weapon which was going to be put into action in the next few hours or days. Besides, the Russians and the Americans would soon start fighting each other. A whispering campaign, cleverly sparked off by Goebbels, had the effect of convincing large numbers of German soldiers fighting outside Berlin that the Americans would soon be joining forces with them against the Russians. Another idea Goebbels had was to drop leaflets over Berlin which said: 'Troops and tanks are on their way to bring us freedom and victory.' This too gave both Berliners and soldiers fresh hope. The army probably referred to here, the Twelfth Army, called 'Wenck' after its Chief, the General of the Tank Troops, was unquestionably too weak for the front. Most of its divisions only existed on paper. Only three of them, which together formed one corps, had produced full numbers. The leader of this Twentieth Army Corps was Köhler, the cavalry general who had told me two weeks before when he presented himself to the General on his return from Norway, that he had just heard that his only son had been killed in battle. He reported that his divisions were very badly equipped and armed. Nearly 90 per cent of the men had no combat experience; they were seventeen- and eighteen-year-olds, fresh from fatigue squads or from officers' training courses. There were some groups where less than half the men were armed. This was the army which was meant to free Germany. When Hitler handed it over to General Wenck at the beginning of April, he had said with great pathos: 'Wenck, I am putting the fate of Germany into their hands.'

Hitler's plan in setting up this army had been to put it into action against the English and Americans. Wenck's mission, according to Hitler's original instructions, was to approach from the area east of the Harz and link up with Army Group B, which was cut off in the Ruhr pocket. Then, when events in the west moved faster than had ever been foreseen, and the Allies cut off the Eleventh Army in the Harz, Wenck was ordered to fight a way through for this army. There was no longer any point in making a sortie towards Army Group B – at this stage it was only a question of how many days the Ruhr pocket could manage to survive.

On 20 April, Hitler's fifty-sixth birthday, the Russians advanced from the Lausitz towards the north-west and by evening had already got as far as the Spreewald. At this point, General Krebs sent the 'escort squadron', the last personal fighting reserve unit at the disposal of the Chief of the Army General Staff, consisting of an augmented, 250 strong, well-equipped motorized reconnaissance squadron, to confront the enemy at Luckau, about 40 kilometres south of our headquarters.

Soon after this, news of a much graver nature came in.

The Russians north of Berlin had pushed forward via Eberswalde and reached Oranienburg. This advance had actually been made on the previous day, but it had been reported only as a breakthrough of 150 Russian tanks. It was in fact, the decisive breakthrough by Marshal Zhukov's tank corps.

Meanwhile, in the Reich Chancellery, the birthday congratulations were going on. On Hitler's birthday this year, almost all his former comrades appeared: they included Göring, Himmler, Bormann and Speer as well as the heads of the three Armed Forces. The day began in a semblance of calm, but very soon Hitler's associates began to urge him to leave Berlin and transfer his staff and headquarters to Upper Bavaria. The only one who did not press him to leave was Goebbels, who was *Gauleiter* and Defence Commissar of Berlin. Hitler could not make up his mind. The only thing to which he would agree, should Germany be split in two by the Russians and Americans meeting, was that Grand Admiral Dönitz should take over control of the independent, northern half of the Empire. As he did not name anyone for the southern half, it must be assumed that at this point he was still toying with the idea of going south himself. Himmler and his staff, as well as the Foreign Affairs Ministry, were to go north to Dönitz; Göring was to go south.

The basic reason, as he so frequently emphasized, why Hitler wanted to remain in Berlin and would possibly continue to do so, was his unshakeable belief in himself. He believed that, inspired by his presence, the spirit of those who were fighting for him would be constantly kindled to heroic efforts which would stand proof against the onslaught of the enemy. Around noon, he presented Iron Crosses to boys of the Hitler Youth who had distinguished themselves by their bravery. It was only in the evening when the guests had left that the full gravity of the report from the front that day was revealed to him. He was told that the Russians had broken through even farther from the Muskau–Forst area, subsequently advancing to the north-west, and Zhukov's tanks lying north of Berlin had succeeded in pushing through to Oranienburg. This spelt utter disaster for the Germans, illustrating as it did that the Russians were setting up a pincer movement to encircle Berlin. Added to this, the Russians were launching an attack on the Third Tank Army's Front. By evening, Marshal Rokossovski's troops had succeeded in building two bridgeheads on this side of the Oder at a point, south of Stettin, where the river had flooded over an area almost three kilometres wide. At this military conference Hitler was also told that, because of the Russian breakthrough to Oranienburg, *Waffen* SS General Steiner had reassembled his troops on the open south flank of the Third Tank Army. In actual fact, this was as yet mere speculation. It is true that Steiner had received instructions to this effect from Army Group Weichsel but he had no troops with which to execute the order. He was meant to assemble these himself from soldiers returning from the front, and it was hoped that as soon as possible the Army Group would send him one or two units.

Hitler sent instructions to Steiner to attack in the direction of Berlin within twenty-four hours at the latest so as to cut off the Russian troops which had broken through north of Berlin from their forces to the rear, and then to wipe them out. His idea in this was still based on retaining the Oder as the backbone of a defence to the east. Parts of the Ninth Army which were still stationed at Frankfurt on the Oder were to launch an attack towards the south and Field-Marshal Schörner was to lead the attack with parts of his Army Group *Mitte*, in this way cutting off Marshal Konyev's troops, who were attacking on the Neisse, from their forces to the rear. All this, Steiner's attack, that by the Ninth Army and that by Schörner's troops was meant to bring about a decisive defeat for the Red Army.

The truth is that Hitler no longer knew, nor did he want to know what was going on outside the Reich Chancellery. When this conference was over and the night of 20 April had set in, the great migration from Berlin began. Himmler and his staff transferred north, Göring and his Air Force Operations Staff, with the exception of Generals Koller and Christian who remained behind for the time being, moved south. With them went the bulk of the Party and Government administration.

At six o'clock the following morning, I was woken by a telephone call from First Lieutenant Kränkel, leader of the squadron which had been sent on a reconnaissance mission the previous day. Kränkel himself was on the line: 'About forty Russian tanks have passed us as well as mounted infantry. I shall go into the attack at 7 o'clock.' We knew then that the headquarters were doomed. There were no reserves left. Wenck's army, which might have saved the situation, was still on the Elbe, fighting the Americans. At 9 o'clock a second call came from Kränkel: 'My own attack has failed with heavy losses. My reconnoitring tanks report further enemy tanks advancing north' – in other words, heading for Berlin and taking in Zossen on the way. I passed on this alarming news to Krebs, who immediately reported it to the Reich Chancellery. This time, he insisted on a decision as to where we should move our headquarters, pointing out the impossibility of directing further operations otherwise. But Hitler still hesitated. On the twenty-second, bad news poured in from both north and south fronts. It spread like wildfire through headquarters, and I hardly had a chance to put the

118

telephone down. Everyone wanted to know whether, in view of the grave news, there would still be a conference that day. My reply was always the same: 'At 11 am as usual.' However, contrary to my chief's orders, I issued instructions for everything to be prepared for a hasty evacuation.

Shortly before the conference began, my room was buzzing with noise and activity, orderlies, clerks and ordinance officers coming and going, generals and colonels talking so loudly that I had to ask them several times to be quiet so that I could hear what was being said on the telephone. But a few minutes before 11 o'clock, the room suddenly became deathly silent. There it was again, that hoarse, barking report that anyone who has ever been out there at the front knows only too well. We all looked at each other more in dismay than astonishment, until someone broke the silence: 'That must be the Russian tanks at Baruth, that's ten or perhaps even fifteen kilometres from here, I think. They could well be here in half an hour.'

General Krebs came out of his room: 'If you're ready, gentlemen.'

The last conference with the Chief of the Army General Staff had begun. It had only just started when I was called out of the briefing to speak to First Lieutenant Kränkel who had turned up at headquarters, exhausted and covered in mud. He reported that all that remained of his squadron was a few vehicles and about thirty or forty men. Baruth had been taken by the Russians. Two of our anti-aircraft guns, about fifty soldiers and a few *Volksstrum* men were still there. The Russians had come to a halt. At the end of his report, he asked if I had any further orders for him.

'Yes,' I said, 'keep yourself, your men and your vehicles ready for action.' Then I returned to the conference room and reported to the General, who immediately telephoned through to Hitler to press urgently for permission to transfer headquarters. But Hitler refused. There was only one thought written on the faces of all the officers as they took their leave: a Russian prisoner-of-war camp.

A short while later, we received a call from Burgdorf. Hitler had ordered all troops still fighting on both sides of the Elbe between Dresden and Dessau-Rosslau to withdraw to Berlin as soon as it was dark, so that the field would be clear for the Americans and the Russians to meet.

But, as so often in that war, the Russians stayed put where we least expected them to. Not finding any opposition worth speaking of, their tank formation sat tight in Baruth, about fifteen kilometres from our headquarters. At last, at about 1 pm Hitler's order came through to move headquarters to the Air Force barracks at Potsdam-Eiche. At the same time, we were told that a military conference would be held in the Reich Chancellery as early as 2.30 pm. Preparations for the move had to be made at top speed. Telephone lines were hurriedly dismantled, and at 2 pm I drove through the main gate of 'Maybach II' in the Potsdam direction, accompanied by the convoy of the Chief of General Staff's military administration section. The Chief and his adjutant had left for Berlin fifteen minutes before.

On the main highway hundreds of thousands of people were on the move, many with horses and carts, others with bicycles, handbarrows or prams, most of them on foot, all heading west, anywhere to escape from the enemy. Tank barricades on the exit routes of the towns and villages only let a trickle through at a time. Here and there above us, on the huge barricades built of wood and stone children were playing, unsuspecting and ignorant of the danger. They waved to us, wearing paper helmets and brandishing wooden swords. Winding our way though the stream of refugees, we pressed on to Potsdam. A motor-cyclist coming in the opposite direction reported that the centre of Berlin was already under artillery fire from the Russians. The first deaths had already been reported in the Dorotheenstrasse, in the centre of the city.

At that very moment, in the Reich Chancellery, the last conference with the Führer was being held. Unfortunately, I could not be there as I had to supervise the transfer of the military administration section, but I heard about it as soon as Freytag-Loringhoven, and later on General Krebs, returned from the conference. Hitler had assembled together for the last time as many representatives of the Armed Forces, the Party and the Government as were still in or near Berlin. And on this 22 April the conference in the Reich Chancellery began just as it always had. Jodl and Krebs gave their reports. It was not until Krebs started talking about the combat areas between the Sudeten and the Stettiner Haff, south and north of Berlin, that Hitler began to take an active interest. By now, immediately south-west of Berlin, the Russian attacking force had reached a line east of Treuenbrietzen–Beelitz–Teltov. In the north of the city fighting was going on in the surburbs of Lichtenberg, Niederschönhausen and Frohnau. Enemy tanks were rolling into the Prenzlauer Allee. The Russian attack north of the city extended over to the west, taking in Oranienburg. Thus it could be only a question of a day or two before Berlin was completely encircled.

At this point Hitler interrupted the report and asked where SS General Steiner and his attacking forces were. He had interrupted because no mention had been made of the order he had given on 20 April to attack the deep flank of the Russian V formation threatening Oranienburg. It was only with some hesitation that Hitler was told that this attack had never even begun, and that it was because those units had been withdrawn from Berlin to support Steiner's forces on Hitler's instructions that the Russians had been able to break through the weakened front line north and north-east of the city and penetrate the outer suburbs of Berlin.

That was too much for him. Hitler interrupted and requested everyone present at the conference, except Keitel, Krebs, Jodl, Burgdorf and Bormann to leave the room. There was a tense and pregnant silence. Then, as if driven by some strange force, Hitler leapt up and began to rant and rave. He turned alternately deathly pale and purple in the face, shaking in every limb. His voice cracked and he screamed about disloyalty, cowardice, treachery and insubordination. As had frequently happened in the course of previous, less violent fits of rage, he proceeded to hurl reproaches against the Army and the *Waffen* SS. The culmination of his tirade was his refusal to leave Berlin – he would stay with the Berliners, he would lead the battle himself, in person. Any-one who wanted could leave him and leave Berlin. And then, those watching witnessed an incredible and quite unpre-cedented scene. Hitler slowly sank back into his chair and in total contrast to the violence with which it had begun, his outburst ended in complete collapse. Sunk into himself, he sobbed like a small child and, continuing to sob, he admitted for the first time straight out and without making any apolo-gies or excuses: 'It is all over. The war is lost. I shall shoot myself.'

For almost five minutes the men watching him stood in bewildered silence. Jodl was the first to speak. He did so quietly and carefully but firmly, reminding Hitler of his duties towards his people and the Army. The others attemp-ted to comfort him and to give him fresh hope by reminding him of the large areas in both north and south which were still held and still being defended by Germany. Yet even though his loyal supporters and colleagues pleaded with him to move to Berchtesgaden immediately and direct operations from there he still remained obdurate, and he stuck to his decision to remain in Berlin.

Later on he confirmed that Grand Admiral Dönitz was to assume full civil and military authority for the entire northern province. From Berchtesgaden, Keitel and Jodl were to take over the further military control of the German forces still fighting in parts of South Germany, Bohemia, Austria, Croatia and North Italy, although in fact, as things turned out, this proved no longer possible. Hitler's pronouncements about Göring's control of the south were vague and unclear. Lastly, he called in Goebbels to ask him to move into the Reich Chancellery bunker with his wife and children and to issue a proclamation to the people of Berlin telling them that he, Hitler, was in Berlin, directing the battle in person and that he would share the fate of the Berliners. He also directed that Bormann, who had refused to obey Hitler's order to leave Berlin, Burgdorf, Krebs and, of course, Goebbels as well as the liaison officers should stay in the bunker with him.

The decisions reached at this conference were immediately passed on by the liaison officers in person or by telephone to their immediate superiors. In the case of both Göring and Himmler this led to various misunderstandings as subsequent events proved. Keitel and Jodl who, to start with, had refused to leave Hitler, did not, as originally planned, go south immediately but promised Hitler to do everything in their power to personally plan and assist the liberation of Berlin. That same night, Keitel left to join General Wenck and the units of his Twelfth Army. Jodl drove over to Steiner and from there to Krampnitz, where Army High Command had moved, so as to organize as much as possible, particularly the Third Army area, from there. At the same time, Hitler's personal physician, Professor Morell, Admiral von Putt-kamer, Adjutant Julius Schraub and any others who had held minor posts on Hitler's staff left Berlin.

When Hitler's closest colleagues had recovered from their shock at his breakdown, they managed by dint of tireless encouragement to rally his spirits. The credit for this was due primarily to Keitel and Jodl, but also to Bormann and, of course, Goebbels, who was condemned, because of the office he held, to remain in Berlin. Keitel and Jodl pointed out the possibilities which a combined attack by the Ninth and Twelfth Armies would open up as well as the further pos-sibilities of an attack by Steiner and Holste. Another idea of Jodl's was completely to withdraw the forces from their engagements with the Western Allies and concentrate them all in the battle for Berlin.

Once again, Goebbels brought into play his eloquent tongue, and he and Bormann reminded Hitler of the en-ormous strength Berlin still had to offer if it were ruthlessly combed. All this, combined with telephone calls from his supporters who had learnt from the liaison officers of Hitler's breakdown, helped to revive Hitler's strength for the final act of resistance. As a result of those developments, the following orders and instructions followed each other in swift succession during the late afternoon.

'1. The Ninth Army [which was still fighting a desperate battle in the area around Frankfurt and was still in some places holding to the Oder] is to proceed to attack, striking towards the west, while protecting its flanks and rear, and in so doing, it is to link up with Wenck's army.

'2. General Field-Marshal Keitel is to proceed directly to

124

General Wenck's army so as to assess the situation there. He will give the order in person to join up with the Ninth Army and retreat from the Front against the Americans. He will then prepare for an attack on Berlin by thrusting towards Ferch, south-west of Potsdam.

'3. Jodl is to join Steiner and advance the attack on Berlin from the area north of Oranienburg.

'4. Grand Admiral Dönitz is instructed to drop all other engagements and give absolute priority to the decisive battle for Berlin.

'5. Goebbels, in his capacity as Defence Commissary for Berlin, has the authority to employ all his powers to the fullest extent to mobilize all possible forces within Berlin.'

Before driving into Berlin with my convoy, I called a halt once more to allow the vehicles, which were separated by considerable distances, to catch up with each other. Two German fighters passed overhead, flying towards the east. The rumbling from the front was now no more than a distant roll of thunder. Near Potsdam station, we passed about twenty or thirty unexploded bombs which had lain there since the last bombing-raid. We were forced to a reluctant halt on the bridges in front of the old palace, by hundreds of vehicles which had piled up in front of the anti-tank obstacles between the two bridges. I got out and tried to sort out the muddle of agitated men with horses and carts, cursing lorry drivers, and mothers weeping helplessly, carrying their children wrapped in a blanket in their arms, all of them shouting in confusion. We could see sappers working nearby, assembling explosive ammunition and unexploded bombs to blow up the bridges.

At last we got through into the city. We were obliged to

drive along side-streets, for many of the roads were blocked by ruins and bomb craters. The bells of the former Potsdam garrison church where Adolf Hitler had once dedicated his Third Reich and taken a solemn vow, lay shattered on the road among debris and ash. The tall, burnt-out windows of the church stared at us like empty eye sockets. When we reached our destination – the barracks in Potsdam-Eiche – we found advance parties there to receive us, and orders ringing out on all sides. By 8 pm when Freytag-Loringhoven came back, exhausted, from the Reich Chancellery, the most pressing work had been done and we sat down together for a while to discuss the day's events. Everything at Potsdam-Eiche was merely temporary; we knew we should not be staying long. What was to become of the two of us, now that General Krebs had been condemned to stay in the capital, we did not know.

Early next day, news filtered through that the headquarters were to be transferred to Rheinsberg and probably from there towards Lübeck. I had hardly dared to hope for this. Perhaps in a few days I should see my wife and child in Lübeck again. That morning I received my new orders from General Detlevsen, who had been put in command of the defence of General Staff Headquarters. But before I could begin my new assignments, Major von Freytag-Loringhoven received a telephone call from General Krebs in the Reich Chancellery. He was to join him there at once with everything he needed for several days' stay in the Reich Chancellery bunker. The Major and I knew what this meant for him. Saying goodbye was extremely hard for all of us.

As General Detlevsen had ordered, I then assembled a combat force, as far as was possible, sent armoured cars out to reconnoitre, and sealed off the straits at Geltov, Wender and Marquard, west, north and south-west of Potsdam.

Here, too, the stream of refugees was swelling relentlessly.

The roads outside the towns presented an increasingly wretched spectacle. For the first time, there were soldiers among the refugees – at first just one or two, then small groups, then an increasingly large number. Some seemed to know where they were heading but most of them were indifferent; they had been caught up in a headlong flight from the eastern front, and were sunk in total apathy. One could see it in the way they walked, the way they held their heads, and in their eyes. There was also an unending stream of wounded and hastily patched-up men.

At 5 pm, I was to report to General Detlevsen. Very tall and nervous, he rose as I entered the room, gave me his hand and explained in a few brief words: 'General Krebs phoned half an hour ago. You are to leave at once for the bunker at the Reich Chancellery to help Freytag. You are to take your personal possessions with you. I think you realize what this means for you.' He looked intently at me, rested his hand on my shoulder and added: 'When the moment comes and that bunch switch on the gas taps, see to it that you get out of the bunker in time and die a decent soldier's death in the Wilhelmplatz.' He spoke this last sentence more slowly, almost like a father to his son. Then he added one final question: 'Is there anything further I can do for you?'

The room had grown very quiet. I gave him my wife's address, took my leave and left. It was only when I was outside, in the half-light of the long barracks corridor, that the awful significance of his words hit me. For days and weeks previously, I had been right in the thick of events and of feverish activity and I had reacted as we all reacted during the war years on the front; we had not asked why and wherefore, nor what the future held for us, we had not had time for thinking and brooding. It is true that in the early weeks and months of my work in the General Staff Headquarters I had been aware that absolute defeat was inevitable in the not-too-distant future. But now this end stood suddenly and immediately before me. It was a cruel awakening.

Slowly, I collected together a few absolutely necessary personal items, said goodbye to everyone and set off. I left behind my orderly, Gummersbach, whom I had asked to take my last message to my wife. Then, bypassing Potsdam, I proceeded via Nedlitz and Krampnitz into the Heerstrasse. The direct route via Wannsee and Dahlem was no longer passable as it was rumoured that the Russians had already crossed the road at Zehlendorf. Darkness had fallen; the streets were almost deserted; the thunder of the battle for Berlin had almost entirely died away. We hardly saw a soul along the length of the broad east–west axis. Only occasionally a shadow flitted from one cellar to another. The deeper we got into the city, the more lifeless this gigantic metropolis appeared. We reached the Wilhelmplatz without incident and turned into the Vosstrasse. The long frontage of the Reich Chancellery rose up dark and massive against the clear night sky.

5. THE STRUGGLE FOR BERLIN

As we approached the Reich Chancellery the dull burst of a shell shattered the illusion of peace. Everything appeared deserted. In front of the Party entrance lay a pile of rubble from a row of houses which had collapsed on to the street. I ordered the car to stop near the Armed Forces entrance, where several cars were already parked. There was no sign of the sentry who was usually on guard there. The car ramp was wrecked. I gave an involuntary shudder. A hiss and a roar shattered the eerie silence once again, and there was the bursting crash of a heavy shell, which must have landed near the Potsdamer Platz. Beyond the ruins, in the direction of the firing, a faint burning glow grew ever brighter. Only a few minutes later the next shell-burst followed, this time farther away. After a longish hunt I finally found the first sentry. The guards at the entrances had retreated into the protective darkness of the building. An SS man came up to me and asked where I was going; then the NCO on guard duty had me conducted at once to the interior of the bunker under the Reich Chancellery. We used a dimly lit side passage. Armed soldiers were leaning against the walls, some of them smoking, others talking, others crouching down asleep, with their heads lolling forwards. The sound of muffled talking mingled with the monotonous whirring of the ventilators. Eventually we reached the battle headquarters of SS Brigade Leader Mohnke, who until recently had been the leader of an SS division. Now he was the leader of the 'Adolf Hitler Volunteer Corps', which he had assembled a few days before in the Tiergarten, volunteers from all over what remained of the Reich. All in all, this force was about two thousand strong and was intended to form the final ring of defences around the Reich Chancellery. Mohnke was speaking loudly to some SS officers, gesticulating all the time, and issuing orders. Despite the ventilators, the air in the small, bare room was stale and suffocating. Mohnke rang the adjutants' office to check on my orders, and I was then escorted farther into the interior of the bunker by two SS men. Here the dull rumble of shells landing could only be faintly heard.

The bunker rooms seemed more austere and uninviting than ever. The cold, grey, concrete walls exuded the damp, musty smell common to all new buildings. Our path took us through a maze of rooms, all of which were connected to each other by passages or thin steel doors. The musty smell, the confused sound of people talking, the humming of the ventilators pervaded everything like a nightmare. There were, all in all, about fifty to sixty bunker rooms beneath the Reich Chancellery. Six exits led out of this labyrinth, three of them directly into the open air, the rest into the ground floor of the Reich Chancellery and to Hitler's bunker in the garden. Several of the rooms were crammed, ceiling-high, with bread, preserves and other supplies so that it was difficult to get through. Other rooms and passages were full of soldiers, most of them leaning listlessly against the walls. Many of them were just lying or sitting on the bare concrete floor, gun in arm, asleep. They were all tall, strong, young SS men. Their appearance did not exactly suggest that they were inspired by eagerness for battle: they seemed, rather, to be resigned to their fate. During the following few days this impression of their state of mind was reinforced; it was true even of very high-ranking officers.

Finally we reached our destination. Again it was a narrow, musty bunker room, closely packed with clerks, draughtsmen and orderlies. General Krebs was away reporting to Hitler with von Freytag-Loringhoven, so I had to wait, listening to the shells from the Russian artillery landing somewhere in the centre of the city, alternating between a loud bursting noise and a low rumbling. My thoughts revolved around one single question: how long will this business last, and what will the end be like? I had to wait a long time, but eventually Freytag appeared. He seemed even taller in the low room. When he saw me, a smile flitted across his face. I reported for duty, strictly in accordance with regulations, but he shook my hand and said: 'Why don't we drop the formality now? There's no point in it any more.' Then after a pause, he added: 'We're all in the same boat now, my dear fellow. Come with me a minute, and I'll give you an outline of your work straight away; the General won't be back just yet.' We passed through a nicely arranged room, the quarters of General Burgdorf and his adjutant, Lieutenant-Colonel Weiss. Our bunker was separated from this one only by a thin steel door. On the left, beside the door in our room, were two bunk beds, and opposite them were two desks for us. A big curtain divided the room in two; the part behind the curtain was occupied by General Krebs. The walls were grey, bare concrete, as in the other bunkers. Once I had deposited my things and sorted them out, von Freytag-Loringhoven explained to me about the place and the company in which we found ourselves.

In his garden bunker Hitler was provided with a study, a bedroom, two living-rooms and a bathroom. Directly beside this private accommodation was the map room or conference room, with which I was already familiar. The hall outside these rooms served as an ante-room during the conferences in the map room. A small room on this lowest floor of Hitler's bunker was the home of Blondi, Hitler's Alsatian dog and her four puppies. A few steps higher there were some eighteen fairly small rooms and passages housing a telephone exchange; a power house; Dr Stumpfegger, Hitler's surgeon, with two rooms; Dr Goebbels with two rooms, and some of Hitler's guards and personal servants. Four rooms on the upper floor were occupied by Frau Goebbels with her five children. Here too were housed the kitchen, with Hitler's vegetarian cook, Fraulein Manzialy, the dining-room, and some more personal adjutants, servants and orderlies.

This building was connected to the world outside by an air shaft with ventilators, by the staircase leading to the garden and by a passage to the other bunker rooms under the Reich Chancellery, which were much higher up than Hitler's bunker.

At the end of this passage was the Press Office run by Heinz Lorenz. Here too Bormann had his quarters and the rooms for his secretariat, in which his personal adviser, *Standartenführer* Zander, and his secretaries were lodged. The adjacent rooms housed Fegelein, Colonel von Below, Admiral Voss, Ambassador Hewel, Hitler's Army adjutant Major Johann-meier, Hitler's pilot Baur and the second pilot Beetz, plus Goebbels' representative in the Propaganda Ministry, Dr Naumann. Brigade Leader Albrecht shared a room with his half-brother, *Standartenführer* Zander. Also living in this complex were Hitler's private secretaries and a few Intelligence assistants. Somewhat set apart from it was the Armed Forces Intelligence department, plus living quarters for General Burgdorf and his adjutant, Lieutenant-Colonel Weiss, and our room which we shared with General Krebs.

All in all there were 600 to 700 people in the bunkers,

counting sentries, orderlies, clerks, kitchen staff and other servants and also a unit of SS troops in the cellars under the Chancellery.

Ambassador Hewel was the permanent representative of the Foreign Ministry in Hitler's entourage: an amiable, rather corpulent diplomat of not above-average talents who was completely under Hitler's influence. He had lived for a long time on Java as a diplomat, from whence Hitler fetched him back after coming to power. His job was no easy one, for Hitler hardly ever saw his professional diplomats, ambassadors and envoys any more, regarding them as weak-kneed defeatists looking at everything through foreign eyes. He dismissed the warnings in their reports out of hand, in so far as he ever read them at all. The way he rewarded the services of his ambassador in Moscow, Count von der Schulenburg, was typical. Schulenburg had issued repeated warnings against a war with the Soviet Union, and on 25 April 1941 had arranged to see Hitler personally in order to try yet again to dissuade him from a war with Russia. Schulenburg was executed after the assassination attempt on 20 July 1944, although there was never any proof of his involvement in the plot.

Admiral Voss was the representative of the Grand Admiral, replacing Admiral von Puttkamer, who had held this post from 1934 until he had been ordered to Berchtesgaden. Major Johannmeier was the successor of the Army adjutant Borgmann, who had been killed a few weeks before by dive-bomber fire while on his way to take over a division in the west.

My assignment here in the bunker was to survey the military situation in and around Berlin and Potsdam hourly, and to prepare reports on it. Bernd – this was von Freytag-Loringhoven's Christian name – was himself to deal with all the other battle areas where German soldiers were still fighting. To bring me up to date Bernd next recounted for me the military developments of the last twenty-four hours.

South of Berlin the Russians were advancing from Jüterbog in the direction of Wittenberg. The Russian spearhead which the day before had advanced to a rough line Treuenbrietzen – Beelitz – Teltow – had moved farther forward to a point south of Potsdam and south-east of Brandenburg. The bulk of the Ninth Army was still in the square formed by Lübben, Guben, Frankfurt an der Oder and Fürstenwalde. There was fighting on the Teltow Canal, south of Berlin. In the suburbs east and north-east of the city, battles were going on everywhere. We had blocked the Russian incursion on the Prenzlauer Allee. We were still holding a position on the Havel, but for how long?

The battle commandant of Berlin, General Reimann, had been relieved of his duties that day by Hitler and replaced by the twenty-seven-year-old Lieutenant-Colonel Bärenfänger, who held the Knight's Cross with oak leaves and swords. In the present situation Reimann had not been tough enough nor unscrupulous enough for Hitler, or even more important, for Goebbels. The original division of Greater Berlin into three defence zones, which General Reimann had drawn up, was already out of date. In these three defence zones – the 'Berlin ring' with a perimeter of 120 kilometres; the line of defence along the Berlin city boundary with a front of about 90 kilometres; and the defence zone along the ring formed by the city railway – the people of Berlin had dug trenches and erected barriers before the Russian attack on 16 April. These pathetically puny defences had not presented the Red Army with any difficulties worth mentioning. Now only one link with the outside world remained open, one single road to the north-west, though Nauen. It was reckoned that the encirclement of Berlin would be complete by the next day, 24 April.

General Wenck's Twelfth Army was in the process of regrouping for a change of front, from the west, in the battle against the Americans, to the east against the Red Army. The most northerly corps of the Army, the Twelfth Tank Corps under General Hoste, was holding on with weakened forces in the area of Rathenow and Plaue. The Twentieth, the most southerly corps, under General Köhler, which with three divisions was the most effective fighting unit in this army, was positioned to the west of the line Wittenbert–Belzig. This army, with its depleted numbers and its shortage of vehicles, tanks, guns and means of communication was not an army at all, in the traditional sense of the word. But, once united with the elements of the Ninth Army left in the region west of Frankfurt an der Oder, it was supposed to be going to liberate Berlin. In Berlin itself the Fifty-Sixth Tank Corps which, under General Weidling had fought its way back from the Oder and was now completely exhausted, was still available for the defence of the city, as well as the remains of routed and shattered divisions from the Oder front anti-aircraft units and the *Volkssturm*. The major element in the defensive forces, however, was the *Volkssturm*, which for its own part was poorly equipped and scarcely worth consideration as a fighting force. There was hardly any artillery available on the 120-kilometre-long front, and there were no reserves of ammunition for the few guns which were available. The much depleted ranks of soldiers were likely to be made up in the next few days by the Hitler Youth, and then, in the city itself there were still something like two million civilians. There was also another weak corps with two divisions in Potsdam, command of which had been taken over that day by General Reimann; in the entire city there were still about forty to fifty tanks available. To face these forces the Russians had assembled four Armies and several thousand tanks and armoured vehicles!

'How long do you think the battle here will last?' I asked Bernd.

His reply came back promptly: 'Eight, at the most ten days.'

'And what can we hope for from Wenck's Army?'

'Nothing, nothing at all: with the forces they've got and their inadequate equipment it is unthinkable that they could make any appreciable differences to the outcome of the main battles.'

'You think there's absolutely no hope then?'

'None at all, only the possibility of dragging out this struggle for Berlin for a few more days. There might still be just a glimmer of hope perhaps, if it wasn't for Hitler,' he added bitterly. 'Hitler still wants to attack, you know; he still hasn't entirely given up his plan to attack and regain the Oder line later on!'

Although the Führer had conceded once already that the war was totally lost, he still seemed incapable of grasping what was really happening outside the bunker. Since his arrival in Berlin in January he had not once left the Reich Chancellery. It would have been the work of a moment to check the state of affairs for himself, but he didn't want to. He didn't want to destroy his fantasy world by contact with reality. If any of those around him ever found the courage to tell him the truth and thus to shake the foundations of this fantasy, he started to rave. Outside, the German Army and the very foundations of the German State were disintegrating, but Hitler still would not give in, he still wanted to attack. He, Bormann and Goebbels had ordered that soldiers and *Volkssturm* men who retreated or did not believe in victory were to be hanged.

As from that morning, the Berliners and those still living and fighting in the city were deluged with exhortations, orders and appeals in the form of posters, leaflets and loud-speaker announcements cooked up by Bormann and Goeb-bels. It was difficult to grasp, but it appeared that after break-ing down the day before, Hitler had once again found a ray of hope. Could it have been the attacks being mounted, in his imagination, by Steiner, Holste, Wenck, Schörner and Busse, which had inspired him to allow the surrounded city of Berlin and its people to be annihilated? Or was it the sacred promises of Keitel and Jodl which filled him with this frankly incomprehensible, new hope? Perhaps it was simply the irresponsibility and cowardice of a man confronted with the prospect of his own death?

That morning 'flying' military courts, exercising frighten-ingly lawless powers had been set up, drawn from the Berlin offices of the Gestapo, from the security police, the military police, the ordinary police and the political bureaux. They were dim-witted fanatics, who had allowed themselves to be made the willing tools of Goebbels and Bormann. They hanged people quite arbitrarily, tying placards on their vic-tims to say that they were cowards or traitors. Hundreds of officers and men, many of them highly decorated for valour, even generals, simply unable to understand the senseless slaughter and destruction any longer or unwilling to join in it, were strung up on trees, on lamp-posts or in the ruins. Often it was only a momentary mental blank on the part of the victims or a misunderstanding which couldn't be im-mediately cleared up that led, within minutes, to a lynching.

Having adapted myself to the situation as best I could, I set to work, preparing the map for Hitler's morning report. My work was made more difficult by the fact that there had already been three changes of battle commandant for Berlin in the few days of fighting, entailing a complete reorganization of the chain of command each time. After the removal of General Reimann at Goebbels' instigation, the post of Battle Commandant of Berlin had been conferred on a Lieutenant-Colonel Kather. Kather, who was unknown to all of us, must have been a 'Goebbels man'. Rumour had it that he was a fanatical Nazi. He dropped out after being wounded, and so the command passed to Lieutenant-Colonel Bärenfänger. I finally found my own solution to this hampering problem by getting information independently over the telephone from the eight commandants of the eight battle sectors of the city, and not from the central source, the battle commandant for the whole of Berlin.

During the course of that evening I heard about yet another scene of the grotesque drama which was being enacted in the Reich Chancellery. It seemed a radio message had arrived that afternoon from Göring. This message said that he, Göring, had been informed that Hitler in Berlin had been deprived of his freedom of action as Head of State by military developments and that he was therefore transferring the leadership of the State and the Armed Forces to himself, on the basis of the decree of 29 June 1941. If he had not heard from Hitler to the contrary by 10 o'clock on the evening of 23 April, he would assume that this had been confirmed. To avoid this radio message passing through Bormann's hand in the Reich Chancellery before Hitler had a chance to see it, Göring had sent several identical messages to Hitler, to his liaison officer in the Reich Chancellery, Colonel von Below, and to Field-Marshal Keitel. But the very thing he was trying to prevent happened. Bormann was the first to lay hands on the message and he lost no time in delivering it to Hitler with the comment that this ultimatum was an obvious ase of high treason. Göring's message was, in fact, dripping with servility towards Hitler, and its tone was little more han one of enquiry – anything but an ultimatum; none the ess, Bormann managed to convince Hitler. The upshot of his intrigue by Bormann was that on the same evening, in a adio message from Hitler, Göring was relieved of all his offices and posts, expelled from the Party and demoted. n addition, on Bormann's initiative, it was arranged that Göring be arrested immediately by the SS and interned.

Reich Minister Speer, Keitel and Jodl, who spoke to Hitler or the last time that afternoon, when they reported the esults of their reconnaissance trips to the front, were witnes-es of Hitler's hysterical reactions to Göring's message and Bormann's diabolical intriguing.

To replace Göring as Supreme Commander of the *Luft-vaffe*, General Burgdorf recommended to Hitler the com-mander of the Sixth Air Fleet in Munich, Colonel-General Ritter von Greim. Greim was not immediately made fully aware of this decision, but was simply ordered to report to he Chancellery, no reason being given.

I finally finished work at nearly 2 am that night. The battle ectors reported an easing off in the fighting towards evening and an almost complete ceasefire by nightfall. About 5.30 n the morning I was rather rudely awakened by five or six heavy Russian shells landing very near the Reich Chancellery. By 6 the shell-bursts were coming regularly, every three min-utes, as they had done the day before. I had still not finished dressing when Günsche, Hitler's personal SS adjutant, was ent to me by Hitler to find out what the latest position was. When he left I rang up the General Staff officers of the Berlin ectors and of the corps in Potsdam. They all told the same tory. At daybreak, after roughly an hour's bombardment, he Russians had attacked everywhere. A few hours later news reached us that the last main road out of Berlin was threatened by Russian troops. Russian tanks had also appeared in the scrub land between Döberitz and Dallgow. This meant that Berlin was as good as completely surrounded. An underground telephone cable was our last link with the outside world: it remained intact until the morning of 28 April. On this line Bernd telephoned Armed Forces High Command, which had moved, late in the evening of 23 April, to Fürstenberg (60 to 70 kilometres north-west of Berlin) just in time to escape being captured. He was given details about the battle situation in the north and south of Germany, in Bohemia, Curland and the Vistula estuary. Bernd and I reported on the situation to General Krebs, and then the three of us set off shortly before 10.30 for Hitler's bunker.

Because of the piles of rubble our route was diverted through the bunker garage, which was connected to the Vosstrasse by a loading ramp, and then through several passages leading to the long corridor beneath the inner courtyard. Here the thin concrete ceiling had been smashed in several places by earlier bombings, and water was ankle-deep in the poorly lit passage. We proceeded cautiously balancing on unsteady planks. Our route led on through the scullery and two dining-rooms, and thence down to Hitler's bunker. It took about five minutes in all, and during that time our credentials were checked in no less than six different places by sentries on duty in pairs, or in threes, armed with machine-guns and hand grenades. In the dining-rooms SS officers and NCOs were sitting at long tables drinking brandy and real coffee with big plates of open sandwiches in front of them. We Army officers received scarcely a nod from these gentlemen. In the ante-room to the conference room in Hitler's bunker we were received by Günsche. Hitler was just finishing breakfast, he said, would we mind having a moment's patience? Outside, in the wide passage leading to the ante-room there were another five, heavily-armed SS officers of the Escort Detachment. I couldn't help thinking how yesterday, up in the Vosstrasse, there had not been a single sentry in evidence. Where was the enemy? In the streets of Berlin or here below in Hitler's bunker?

There was some attempt at decoration in the small ante-room. On the long wall on the right-hand side was a brown bench over which hung six smallish paintings, old Italian masters. Along the opposite wall stood a table with a bench and four rustic-style chairs. To the right of this a door led into the conference room, to the left was the door to Hitler's apartment.

Soon this left-hand door opened, and Hitler appeared; behind him Goebbels limped in, and then came Bormann. Hitler shook hands with Krebs and then with us and walked the few feet to the conference room. His posture was more bent than ever, his gait still more shuffling. The old flicker in his eyes, which I had found so unnatural, had disappeared. Now his features were all flaccid, and he looked exactly like a sick old man. Krebs stood to the left of Hitler's chair, Goebbels opposite him. This small, gaunt man had broken down too; he looked pale and hollow-cheeked, his expression betraying deep disquiet. He followed our reports precisely on the map, asking only the occasional question. The movements of his features and his once so fanatical eyes betrayed anxiety. His post as Defence Commissary of Berlin tied him and his family to the city, so that he had now become the prisoner of his own propaganda. The others had at least taken their families to safety, but he was compelled to share his death with a wife and five children.

I had to leave the room briefly to take a telephone call. When I returned, Hitler was still talking to Krebs, and Goebbels slipped quietly out from behind the table, came over to me and asked in a whisper what news there was. He didn't seem to expect anything good. I told him in a whisper, that the Russians had advanced with their armoured divisions from the bridgehead at Gartz, to the south of Stettin, and had gained 50 kilometres of territory to the west. What defences we had left there were very thin.

Krebs had finished making his report. Hitler looked up at me questioningly. I hesitated; I would have preferred Krebs to go first in outlining the situation, but he made a gesture of refusal, so I had to report the facts to Hitler myself. Throughout, my attention was distracted by the marked shaking of his head. Whenever his quivering hand reached out or moved around on the map, I had to pull myself together sharply for fear of losing the thread of my argument. When I had finished, he reflected for a moment and then turned to Krebs and began to shout at him in a blustering voice. His body was bent right over, his hands convulsively gripping the arm-rests of the chair. He spoke disjointedly, illustrating his words with gestures and directions on the map: 'In view of the broad natural barrier formed by the Oder, the Russian success against the Third Tank Army can only be attributed to the incompetence of the German military leaders there.' Krebs tried cautiously to object that we only had inadequately equipped emergency units and *Volkssturm* forces in this area, whereas Marshal Rokossovsky had at his disposal first-rate Russian crack divisions. He pointed out too that the reserves of the Third Tank Army under General von Manteuffel had already been thrown in on the hard-pressed right wing and the exposed right flank of the Army or been moved back to Berlin. But Hitler dismissed these objections irritably with a wave of his hand: 'The attack from the north of Oranienburg must be initiated tomorrow at the latest. The

Third Army will make use of all available forces for this offensive, ruthlessly depleting those sections of our front line which are not under attack. It is imperative that the link to Berlin from the north be restored by tomorrow evening. Have that passed on at once.' Bernd left the room, to pass on this order, and Burgdorf, who had joined us in the meantime, said something, in passing, about *Waffen* SS General Steiner leading this attack north of Oranienburg. Until recently Steiner had been the leader in Curland of the Third Germanic SS Corps, a really élite unit; and he had been a particular protégé of the SS and of Hitler. But now Hitler seemed about to have one of his uncontrollable fits of rage: 'Those arrogant, boring, indecisive SS leaders are no good to me any more,' he barked. 'I do not wish Steiner to continue in command there under any circumstances.' He ordered that command of the attack be taken away from him at once, and ended the conference.

Towards midday news reached us that pressure on the city had increased considerably from the south. Barely an hour later we were notified that Tempelhof airport was under fire from Russian artillery and could not be used any longer. From then on the Gatow airfield had to cope with the entire operation of supplying Berlin from the air. But by about 5 o'clock Gatow airfield too was reported under fire.

Soviet infantry had appeared in the heathland to the north of Döberitz. Three T34s were already blocking the Berlin–Nauen road, the last main road out of the city to the west. As a desperate measure work had been going on since around midday to convert the east–west thoroughfare on both sides of the Victory Column in the centre of Berlin, into a landing and take-off strip. Towards evening shelling of the city centre intensified considerably. During the last few days the shelling seemed to have been intended only as a nuisance, probably coming from a single 17.5 battery; but now the shells were being fired at short intervals, suggesting that the Russians had already brought up their artillery in pretty large quantities. Later that evening news reached us via the Staff of Army Group Vistula that the Ninth Army was involved in a rigorous defensive action on the line Lübben–Guben–Frankfurt–Fürstenwalde: this made it almost impossible for them to carry out the order to regroup for attack in the west and join up with Wenck's Army. The Russian spearhead south of Berlin had now reached the region south of Potsdam and south-east of Brandenburg. From the Twelfth Army we received news that they had so far been unable to form a solid defensive front or to make any concentrations of troops in preparation for an assault on Berlin. The units of the Twentieth Corps, on the other hand, had split up into combat groups and were engaging the forward units of the attacking Russian forces.

During the night of 24 April Hitler decreed the disbandment of Army High Command and its integration into Armed Forces High Command, as well as the fusion of the General Staff of the Army with the Staff of the Armed Forces Headquarters under the command of Jodl, who had thus finally achieved his ambition, albeit rather late in the day.

On the evening of the twenty-fourth there was an unconfirmed report that near Ketzin, some fifteen kilometres to the north-west of Potsdam, forward units of Marshal Konyev's Army approaching Berlin from the south had for the first time met units of Marshal Zhukov's Army, approaching from the north.

At midnight on 24 April our final impression of the battles in the area of the city was that our own resistance had in fact been somewhat stiffened by the draconian measures of the military courts and the ruthless recruiting of Goebbels and

Bormann on 24 April. But our suspicion that the Russians had already brought up their artillery was confirmed on the following day, 25 April. Dead on 5.30 in the morning there began the heaviest bombardment of the city centre yet. It continued for nearly an hour before it eased off again to the familiar pattern of nuisance fire. We were ordered, shortly before 10.30, to make a report to Hitler. On our arrival in the ante-room we found Bormann and Lorenz already waiting there, and after a brief exchange of greetings, during which Hitler joined us, we moved into the conference room to hear the latest reports. Before Krebs could begin his remarks, Lorenz intervened and asked to be allowed to speak.

Using his radio equipment in the Propaganda Ministry he had picked up the following news in the early hours of the morning from a neutral radio station. When American and Russian troops had met for the first time near Torgau on the Elbe in central Germany, there had been minor differences of opinion between the commanders of the American and Russian units over the sectors to be occupied. The Russians complained that in this area the Americans had not observed the agreements reached at Yalta. That was all there was to it: there was absolutely nothing to suggest a bloody end to the argument or anything like that.

But Hitler seemed electrified by this news; his eyes were shining again, and he sat back erect in his chair.

'Gentlemen, here again is quite striking evidence of the disunity of our enemies. Would not the German people and posterity brand me a criminal if I were to make peace today when there is still the possibility of our enemies falling out amongst themselves tomorrow? Is it not possible that on any day, even at any hour, war will break out between the Bolsheviks and the Anglo-Saxons over Germany, their prize?'

I was reminded of the way Hitler put this point when much later, after the war, I spoke to an officer who had taken part in the negotiations for unconditional surrender in Rheims on 6 May 1945. He told me the following story. The German delegation had already arrived in Rheims. The negotiations could not begin without General Eisenhower, who came later than the rest. Immediately after his arrival Eisenhower went over to Jodl and, once brief introductions had been made, addressed the following question to him: 'Why did you carry on fighting in 1944 after the defeat at Avranches? You must have known that at least from that moment on the fight was clearly decided in our favour?'

Jodl's reply was: 'Hitler and I were of the opinion that our adversaries would quarrel over plundering Germany and on ideological grounds.'

When Hitler had finished, he turned back to Krebs. In the course of our reports he enquired several times about the whereabouts of General Wenck's troops and about the outcome of the attack on Berlin from the north which the Third Army had been ordered to mount. But there was nothing new whatsoever to report about either of these concerns. It was on that day that our telephone link with the outside world first began to be disrupted. We had, as yet, no radio link, so for some hours we were completely unable to receive news from outside. The Russian artillery fire was increasing almost hourly: during the afternoon the Reich Chancellery received its first direct hits from heavy Russian shells. For a quarter of an hour the ventilators had to be turned off, because they were drawing sulphur stench, smoke and limestone dust into the interior of the bunker, instead of fresh air.

During the afternoon and early evening reports of worsening conditions followed thick and fast, one after another.

In the afternoon the Armed Forces High Command in Furstenberg reported the total collapse of the Oder Front between Gartz and Stettin. Strong armoured units from Marshal Rokossovsky's Army had advanced westwards from the Oder on a broad front, striking towards Neustrelitz and Neubrandenburg.

There was also bad news about the relief attack on Berlin from the position north of Oranienburg – the attack which Hitler had ordered. Although we had gained some two kilometres of territory and had formed a smallish bridgehead south of the Ruppin Canal, the attack had then ground hopelessly to a halt, with extremely heavy casualties, in the face of overwhelmingly superior numbers.

From the Twelfth Army there were reports of strong enemy attacks on the line Wittenberg–Treuenbrietzen. In the early hours of the morning the High Command of this Army announced that three divisions of the Twentieth Corps had been successfully assembled under General Köhler in the area south-west of the line Niemegk to Belzig. However, these operations were being badly hampered by the vigorous Russian attacks. The Twelfth Army was still hoping to break out from the assembly area with these three divisions and to attack in the direction of Beelitz and Trebbin, i.e. to meet the Ninth Army.

Russian pressure westwards in the area west of Berlin had greatly increased. As a result, we in Berlin were moving farther and farther into the 'Russian hinterland'. The morale of many of us in the bunker of the Reich Chancellery reached an absolute nadir when it became known that just before 6 o'clock the Russian forward units in the southern districts of the city had penetrated right up to Zehlendorf and deep into Neukölln. Fighting was in progress on the Teltow Canal to the south of Dahlem. Vehicles from a Russian reconnaissance group had appeared – although only briefly – on the Gatow airfield. The 2000 men of the neighbouring Kladow school of aerial warfare dug in around the precincts of the school. For all practical purposes, therefore, the Gatow airfield was out of use. Hitler commanded that Berlin be supplied by air-drops during the night. We were again ordered to report to him for an interim assessment of the situation about 7 o'clock. He was very dejected. Even the fact that Steiner had led the attack north of Oranienburg, in defiance of his express orders, did not provoke him to one of his notorious emotional outbursts, as we had expected. He merely commented wearily: 'I told you so; under Steiner's command the whole attack was bound to come to nothing.'

As the Russian attack at Spandau constituted the most immediate threat to the defences in the west of Berlin, Reich Youth Leader Axmann received orders to mobilize the Hitler Youth and to send them into action *en masse* at this spot. The Spandau bridges over the Havel at Pichelsberg were to be held at all costs; this was described as the principal task of the Hitler Youth in the struggle for Berlin. During the fighting in and around Berlin Axmann had left the Reich Youth building on the Adolf Hitler-Platz and had set up his command post near the Reich Chancellery in the Wilhelmstrasse. He appeared daily at the Reich Chancellery to report or to be brought up to date on the situation. Otherwise, when during the next few days his boys were thrown relentlessly into the hopeless fight, he stayed with them almost constantly.

The news about our rapidly deteriorating situation naturally spread like wildfire in the bunker. SS leaders of Hitler's Escort Detachment, who previously had scarcely noticed us or had treated us only with condescension, suddenly became friendliness itself. Bernd and I found it difficult to avoid the many questions which met us at almost every corner of the bunker. 'When do you think Wenck will get to Berlin?' 'Can we break out to the west?' 'How much longer can we hold out?' These men, who had always been supercilious and arrogant towards us Army officers were now looking to us for comfort and confidence. For the most part the questions came from men who had no experience of the front, and had never been face to face with death. Some of them drank themselves into insensibility and drifted dazedly towards the unknown. The forced inactivity in the bunker, whilst the shells were bursting over our heads, was bound to have a demoralizing effect on them. Many of them first realized that evening that the bunker would be their grave. And yet it did not seem to occur to any of them to volunteer for action in battle.

Later in the evening I rang up the staff officers of the eight battle sectors and asked them about the morale of the troops – something not mentioned in the daily reports. The picture was the same everywhere. Many of the old *Volkssturm* soldiers, almost all of them inadequately armed, trained and equipped, and convinced of the futility of the fighting in their city, were leaving their positions at the approach of even relatively light Russian forces and trying to escape to join their wives and children in the cellar of their houses. Most of them had only responded to the call-up in the first place out of fear of the flying courts-martial of the SS and the military police. The regular troops, what few of them were left, fought hard but had scarcely any ammunition left. Worst of all was the lack of trained and experienced soldiers, which became more glaring with ever hour. Whilst the front had withstood attack in some places, in others the

Russians had met virtually no resistance at all, and they were able to march in to the rear of those soldiers still putting up a fight. All sectors had had great difficulty coping with the supply situation and with the roaring fires in the city. As there was no water to put the fire out, it raged unimpeded through whole rows and streets of houses. Only ruins, where there was nothing left to burn, could contain the fire now. The Russian superiority in equipment, especially in tanks and artillery, was overwhelming. Our aircraft could not be used to any effect in this maze of walls. An officer reported from one of the southern sectors of the city that former German prisoners of war, members of the 'National Committee', were rendering the Russians invaluable service as guides. I reported all this to the General.

It had grown very late, and Bernd and I went upstairs and out into the open air. The noise of battle had almost died away, only a few solitary shells could be heard dully a fairly long distance off. Fires shed an orange glow on the darkness but the air was clean and cool and we took deep pleasure in filling our lungs after so long underground. A beautiful expanse of starlit sky stretched over the sorely-tried city. For a long time we stood staring silently into the intermittent glow of the fires. Finally Bernd said: 'In a few days all this will be over. I don't want to die with that lot down there in the bunker. When it comes to the end, I want my head above ground and free.' Then he fell silent again, but what he had said weighed heavily on our thoughts. Towards midnight we went back into the bunker, where we still had a pile of work to get through.

Around 8 o'clock on the next morning, 26 April, reports came in from several sectors about supplies dropped from the air. At first light a group of *Messerschmitt* 109s had dropped several hundred canisters of supplies on the centre of the city. Unfortunately, in the vast heaps of debris only about a fifth of them had been found. As far as ammunition was concerned this was merely a drop in the ocean. The worst shortage of ammunition was felt by the few tanks still available and the artillery of the Fifty-Sixth Tank Corps, which could not even be brought into action properly, for lack of ammunition. We sent a radio message to Armed Forces High Command, ordering that transport planes were to land, regardless of risk, on the east–west thoroughfare and fly ammunition into the city. The lamp-posts and trees in the way had been removed several days before, to create a satisfactory runway. And by 9.32 we received confirmation that two *Junker* 52s with tank ammunition had taken off. I passed this message on to the appropriate sectors at once, to prevent any confusion. At the same time the military casualty units set up in the Charité hospital were given instructions to have fifty wounded ready for flying out in about two hours. At 10.30 the two aircraft landed smoothly in the vicinity of the Siegessäule. The effect of this on us all was indescribable. We had grown modest in our expectations, and it was after all at least the semblance of a link with the outside world. At 11 o'clock both aircraft were loaded with severely wounded and made ready for take-off. Everything was done in feverish haste, as it was of course vital not to expose the planes to artillery fire for a second longer than was absolutely necessary. The first aircraft did, in fact, manage to take off without a hitch. The second *Junker* 52, however, brushed its left wing against the undemolished front of a ruined building and crashed shortly after take-off. I later learned that not all of the passengers in this plane lost their lives, thanks to the fact that the plane was still low and flying pretty slowly when the accident occurred.

At 8 o'clock, after a heavy bombardment, the Russians

attacked the Teltow Canal between Dreilinden and Teltow. Here too our defences were overrun very quickly. By the evening the districts of Machnow, Nikolassee, Zehlendorf, Schlachtensee and Steglitz were entirely in Russian hands. In Neukölln there was fighting on the southern perimeter of the Tempelhof airfield. The Russian plan to push deep into the Grunewald forest with motorized units was thwarted on the narrow strip of land between Schlachtensee and the Krumme Lanke lake, but the divisions fighting here, the Eighteenth and Twentieth *Panzer* Grenadier divisions, were in a desperate plight.

The reports from the battle sectors in the eastern and northern parts of the city were just as devastating as those from the south. The enemy had attacked here also after a short but intensive bombardment. In the course of the day there was stubborn fighting with heavy casualties near the Stettiner Station and the Görlitz Station. We completely lost control of the Weissensee, Reinickendorf and Tegel districts. A particularly grave development was a Russian advance to Siemensstadt, which was only halted on the banks of the Spree, where bitter fighting was still going on. Towards evening the first fighting in Charlottenburg was reported.

As our information from the various districts of the city grew increasingly unreliable and contradictory, we had to try to put together our own picture of the situation, at first hand. We decided to use the still relatively intact Berlin telephone network. We simply rang the numbers of acquaintances in streets and districts where we knew that fighting was going on, or thumbed through the telephone book and chose suitable addresses and numbers at random which, from their location, seemed likely to yield the information we needed. This may have been a pretty primitive form of reconnaissance for the Supreme Command of the German Army, but it did, in fact, bring the desired results.

'Excuse me, madam, have you seen the Russians?'

'Yes,' came the frightened reply, more often than we cared to hear; 'half an hour ago two of them were here. They were part of a group of about a dozen tanks at the cross-roads. There has been no fighting here, but about fifteen minutes ago I saw the tanks through my window, driving on in the direction of Ringstrasse.'

I was perfectly satisfied with this information. We fitted together many such conversations and produced a fairly complete picture, which was certainly a lot clearer than the messages from the troops.

6. THE END OF THE SELF-DESTRUCTION

When we went to make our reports to Hitler at 7 o'clock on the evening of 26 April, we found an almost indescribable state of uproar in the ante-room. General Ritter von Greim had arrived from Munich with the woman air-ace, Hanna Reitsch, to report to Hitler, as ordered. Greim had been wounded in the right calf by Russian flak during the flight, and he was lying on a stretcher. While the doctor was still attending to Greim in his surgery Hitler informed him of the reason for his presence in the Chancellery, which hitherto had been a mystery to him. He described the 'treachery' of Reich Marshal Göring, speaking at some length and interlarding his narrative with abuse of his former colleague. Then he promoted Greim to Field-Marshal and appointed him the new Supreme Commander of the *Luftwaffe*.

I suppose there has rarely been a man so surprised at being promoted and appointed to a new post as Greim was on this occasion. It was not only the reason for his promotion and appointment, and the circumstances surrounding it, which were peculiar, but also the fact that he had been dragged away from his military duties to be given this information at the risk of being killed or captured. His flight from Munich to Rechlin, in Mecklenburg, had been extremely foolhardy in view of the absolute air superiority of the enemy, and considering the fact that the territory he had to fly over was almost entirely occupied by the Allies. Greim and his companion had been escorted by *Luftwaffe* fighters as far as the Gatow airfield in Berlin where they had had to land, although the airfield was under artillery fire. They had con-

154

tinued their flight in a slow, *Fieseler Storch* training plane, and during the flight from Gatow into the centre of the city Greim, who had taken the controls himself, had been hit by flak over Russian-occupied Grunewald. When Greim collapsed at the controls Hanna Reitsch had leaned over him and landed the aircraft smoothly near the Brandenburger Tor.

Hanna Reitsch and Hitler were old friends, and they greeted each other warmly. She remained modestly in the background during any discussions, but this pretty woman with her fresh, positive ways commanded the unqualified respect of all those assembled here in the bunker. Two days later Hitler had the foresight to give her a phial of poison. Her only reply was a smile which expressed all her selfless loyalty.

On the way back from the conference to our room we met Frau Goebbels. During the past few days Frau Magda Goebbels, like Hanna Reitsch, had not shown the slightest sign of fear. Her attitude seems incomprehensible unless one remembers her fanatical, almost religious faith in Hitler. How much of it was still genuine by this time, we shall probably never know. One of the more important sources of Hitler's tragic power over the German people was, of course, the hypnotic influence which he had on people, and on women in particular. Around 8.30 Bernd was in touch with Armed Forces High Command. According to the latest radio messages received, forward units of the Ninth Army, attacking from the area of Frankfurt an der Oder, had crossed the Zossen–Baruth road to the south of Berlin. The attack by the Twelfth Army was making only very slow progress in face of stubborn enemy resistance in the wooded country at Beelitz. The next twenty-four hours would show whether there was any chance of success here. There was no further news of Holste's corps or of Steiner's 'attack' near

Oranienburg, but the Russians had succeeded in their drive against the Third Tank Army, advancing from the south of Stettin towards Neubrandenburg and Neustrelitz.

Another conference was summoned towards 11 o'clock that evening. On the way Bernd met Lieutenant-Colonel Weiss behind the scullery. Weiss had just come from Hitler's bunker. I stood waiting at the scullery door and was the involuntary witness of a scene between some kitchen maids and some SS men. The women, real Berliners, poured contempt and scorn on these 'bunker soldiers': 'Listen, if you lot don't pick up your guns and start fighting soon you can put our aprons on and we'll go outside and fight. You ought to be properly ashamed of yourselves; just look at the kids out there smashing Russian tanks. . . .'

General Weidling, the commander of the Fifty-Sixth Tank Corps, who had been highly decorated for valour, was waiting in the ante-room to the conference room. He gave the impression of great vigour despite his fifty-five years of age. Bernd told me that he was to be Battle Commandant of Berlin, he had just heard the news himself from Weiss. Since 23 April this post had been held by young officers who, although they were committed Nazis, did not possess any exceptional military abilities, and had proved unable to cope with the dire situation in Berlin; now, at last, the decision had been made to bring in an experienced general. But Weidling had sufficient sense of responsibility not to accept his appointment without reservations. When Hitler gave him the job of taking over the totally bungled military situation in Berlin, he agreed only on one condition; that nobody from the Reich Chancellery was to interfere with his authority. During the conference that day Hitler agreed, after some hesitation, to respect this qualification.

The next morning, at 6, I was woken by Bernd with some

difficulty. The fresh-air ventilators had temporarily failed and an acrid stench of sulphur, mixed with suffocating limestone dust, filled our room. Outside all hell was let loose. The bunker shook as if it were caught up in an earthquake as shell after shell landed on the Reich Chancellery building. It was about a quarter of an hour before the bombardment eased off and, judging by the noise, moved on towards the Potsdamer Platz.

Reports from the city grew ever worse. The women, old men, invalids, wounded, soldiers and refugees in Berlin had now been living for nearly a week without a break in the cellars and ruins of the city centre. No reasonably organized supply system existed any longer. The thirst was even worse than the hunger, for there had been no water for days. The fires were now quite out of control, belching stifling smoke into the cellars, improvised shelters and passages. And above it all burnt relentless April sunshine. The hospitals, military casualty units and bomb-proof bunkers had long since been filled to overflowing with wounded. Thousands of wounded soldiers and civilians lay in the tunnels and stations of the tubes and the underground: no one will ever know how many there really were. Yet even in this desperate situation some of the men in the bunker still took fresh hope when, at 10.30, news of Wenck's Army was finally picked up again. To the south-west of Potsdam in the extensive woods around Beelitz its forward units had made some further progress towards the Schielowsee. Only a few kilometres separated them from General Reimann's corps, which was fighting near Potsdam. Now the only subject of conversation in the bunker was the short distance between the Twelfth Army and Reimann's corps, and the coming liberation of Berlin by General Wenck. But a few hours later Wenck's Army reported strong Russian attacks on their flank, in the area of the

157

Beelitz sanatoria, and when, in the evening, Wenck had got no farther, and nothing but severe defensive fighting was reported, most people realized that the three divisions were much too weak to push on and fight their way through into the centre of the city. The mood was reversed again, and many were near despair.

That morning I saw Eva Braun, for the first time. She was sitting with Hitler and several of his closest associates at the table in the ante-room, making lively conversation. Hitler was listening to her. She was wearing a close-fitting grey suit, which emphasized a very good figure, and elegant shoes; I was struck too by a pretty, diamond-studded wrist-watch. Undoubtedly an attractive woman, but rather affected and theatrical.

Hitler stood up as we reported, and we followed him into the conference room. Regardless of the absence of any further reports of success from Wenck, he once again clutched at this straw. He wanted to delay the end of the struggle for Berlin still further, without a thought for the thousands, hungry, thirsty or dying in the city. And then came one of the most inhuman of his orders during the last days of the fighting in Berlin. Because the Russians had repeatedly pushed back our front in the city area by advancing through the tube and underground tunnels and thus getting to the rear of the German soldiers, he ordered special units to open the locks of the Spree and flood the tunnels of the underground to the south of the Reich Chancellery. In these tunnels at this juncture there were countless civilians and thousands of wounded. But their lives were of no importance to him, and this insane order caused many deaths.

After the conference we met Hanna Reitsch. She had already made two attempts to take off near the Branden-burger Tor with the wounded Field-Marshal von Greim, but each time she had had to give up because the artillery fire was too heavy. During her stay in the bunker of the Reich Chancellery she had struck up a close friendship with Magda Goebbels, and I often saw them together.

A little later that afternoon some men from Hitler's Escort Detachment brought in a little boy, in a bad state of shock and looking as if he had not slept for days, who had just put a Russian tank out of action near the Potsdamer Platz. With a great show of emotion Hitler pinned an Iron Cross on the puny chest of this little chap, on a mud-spattered coat several sizes too big. Then he ran his hand slowly over the boy's head and sent him back out into the hopeless battle in the streets of Berlin.

Freytag, Weiss and I went back to our bunker rooms together and discussed this unreal scene. We were officers who had seen years of active service, and we found it intolerable to crawl off and hide whilst fighting was going on outside. We did not notice that Bormann had turned up and was listening. Suddenly, with an air of benevolence, he put his hands on Freytag's shoulders and on mine and stepped between us. He got on to the subject of Wenck's troops, the relief of Berlin and the imminent victorious end to the war. Then he added in his unnaturally forced tone: 'When this battle ends in victory for us, as it soon will, you who have been loyal to the Führer and who have shared his darkest hours with him, will hold high offices in the state and will be rewarded for your loyal services with large estates.' Then he smiled graciously at us and went smugly on his way. At first I was so stunned that I couldn't think of anything to say. So it was for manorial estates that we were doing our duty. I wondered if, on this 27 April, he could really be serious about the 'victorious end of the war'? As so often before when I had heard or seen him or Goebbels or Göring or the other men around Hitler, I asked myself if they really believed what they were saying? Or was it a diabolical mixture of pretence, megalomania and fanatical stupidity?

After it was learned late in the evening that spearheads of Wenck's Army had battled their way through to Ferch on the Schielowsee, the Commandant of Berlin asked to be allowed to make a report to Hitler. Bormann, Krebs and Burgdorf stood silently behind Hitler whilst General Weidling reported roughly as follows. Wenck's Army was much too weak, both in men and material, to hold the territory they had just gained to the south of Potsdam, let alone to break through into the centre of Berlin. At the moment the forces of the Berlin garrison were still in a position to make a break-out to the south-west, with some chance of success, with the aim of joining up with Wenck's Army.

'Führer,' Weidling continued, 'I will take personal responsibility for getting you safe and unharmed out of Berlin. The Reich capital would thus be spared the devastating final stages of the battle.' Hitler turned the idea down. Again, on the following morning, when Axmann made the same suggestion and pledged the life of every single member of the Hitler Youth to give the Führer a safe escort, Hitler again refused to leave Berlin.

When news got round the bunker that no significant help could be expected from Wenck's Army and that Hitler had rejected the possibility of a break-out from the city, a sort of doomsday mood spread amongst Hitler's men. We were still hard at work as they attempted to drown their fears in alcohol. The best wines and spirits and foodstuffs were raided from the extensive supplies in the Reich Chancellery. Whilst the wounded in the cellars and the tube tunnels of the city could not even relieve their agonizing hunger and thirst, many of them lying only a few yards away from the Reich

Chancellery in the tube station in the Potsdamer Platz, here the wine was flowing.

About 2 o'clock in the morning I lay down, utterly exhausted from long hours of work, to try to get a few hours sleep. Noise was resounding across from the next room. Bormann, Krebs and Burgdorf were in there, drinking together in animated mood. I must have been asleep for some two and a half hours when Bernd, lying below me in his bed, woke me and said: 'You're missing something, old chap; listen to this a minute. They've been yelling like this for quite a while.' I sat up and listened to what was going on in the next room. Burgdorf was shouting:

'Ever since I took on this job, nearly a year ago, I've put all my energy and idealism into it: I've tried every way I know to bring the Army and the Party closer together and I've been snubbed for my pains, by my former friends in the Services, even despised by some of them. I have done everything in my power to dispel the distrust which Hitler and the Party feel towards the Armed Forces. In the end they accused me in the Forces of being a traitor to the German officer class, and now I can see that those recriminations were justified, that my work was in vain, my idealism wrong – not only wrong, but naive and stupid.'

He paused for a moment, breathing heavily. Krebs tried to calm him down, appealing to him to remember that Bormann was present. But Burgdorf went on:

'Leave me alone, Hans, these things have got to be said some time. In forty-eight hours it will probably be too late. Our young officers went to war with great faith and idealism. Hundreds of thousands of them have gone to their deaths. And for what? For their fatherland, for our greatness and our future? For a decent, clean Germany? In their hearts, yes; but not in reality. They have died for you, for your good living and your megalomania. The youth of a nation of eighty million has shed its blood on the battlefields of Europe, millions of innocent people have been sacrificed, whilst you, the leaders of the Party, have lined your pockets from the wealth of the nation. You have lived well, appropriated huge fortunes, stolen estates, built castles, wallowed in opulence, deceived and oppressed the people. You have trodden our ideals in the dirt, and our morality, our faith, our souls. For you human beings were nothing more than a means of feeding your insatiable lust for power. You have destroyed our culture with its hundreds of years of history, you have destroyed the German people. That is the terrible burden of the guilt you bear!'

The General had shouted these last sentences almost as if he were under solemn oath. It had grown very quiet in the bunker. One could hear him gasping for breath. Then we heard Bormann's voice, cool, deliberate and oily, making this feeble reply: 'There's no need to start getting personal about it, old boy. All the others may have got rich quick, but I am not guilty. That I swear to you by all that's sacred to me. *Prost*, old boy!'

By all that's sacred to me! Yet I knew for certain that he had acquired a large property in Mecklenburg and another in Upper Bavaria, and that he was having a feudal villa built on the Chiemsee. Had he not, only a few hours before, offered us the prospect of large estates? This was the sacred oath of the supreme leader, after Hitler, of the National

Socialist German Workers' Party.

I tried to get to sleep again, but without success. About 5.30 the Russian artillery fire started up again. On this morning of 28 April it escalated very quickly into an intense bombardment, an unending inferno. I had not experienced such a prolonged and intense bombardment of such force during the entire war. The fresh-air ventilators often had to be turned off for a whole hour at a stretch. Several times holes were knocked in the upper levels of the concrete ceiling, and we could hear the heavy lumps of concrete falling on to the lower layer. The dull, heavy explosions of bombs mingled with the bursting of shells, while a hurricane of fire and metal descended on the Reich Chancellery and the surrounding government district. The aerial of our 100 watt radio transmitter was shattered; the lines to various defence sectors in the city were destroyed. The only means of communication which we now had left were runners, and the radio transmitter and receiver operated by Lorenz, the press officer. Again and again we thought that the firing had reached its peak, only to be proved wrong each time. The lack of fresh air in the bunker became unbearable, and headaches, shortage of breath and sweating became increasingly noticeable. Gradually the people in the bunker degenerated into obtuse, aimless brooding. During short breaks in the firing the Russians attacked over and over again. There was fighting on the Alexanderplatz; Russian tanks were approaching the Wilhelmstrasse, and with it the Reich Chancellery, from the direction of the Hallesches Tor. Now only about 1000 metres was left between us. Even the picked men of the SS 'Adolf Hitler Volunteer Corps' could no longer withstand this overwhelming assault.

During the morning and towards midday some of our runners managed somehow to get through to the Battle

Commandant of Berlin and come back alive. The situation was deteriorating in other parts of the front all over the city as badly as it was in our sector of the city centre. Charlottenburg was almost completely lost, and the Russians, approaching from the north, had already reached the east-west thoroughfare at the point called 'the knee'. The backbone of the defence in the inner area of the city now consisted only of the flak towers in the Humboldthain, Friedrichshain and Zoo parks and the anti-aircraft guns on the Shell building. In the areas within range of these 'fortifications' the Russians could make no significant progress. But in other places they were making up for it by penetrating all the farther into the city centre.

The *Fieseler Storch* aeroplane in which Hanna Reitsch and Ritter von Greim had flown into Berlin on 26 April, and in which they had intended to leave Berlin again, was destroyed by the heavy bombardment during the morning.

Care of the wounded was becoming increasingly difficult in all sectors. There was a growing shortage of doctors, of bandages, of drugs and medicines, but most of all of water.

When I went downstairs about midday with the papers for the conference, I was confronted by a bizarre, almost comic spectacle. Following their impassioned nocturnal argument, Burgdorf, Krebs and Bormann had moved from their previous living and working quarters into the little ante-room outside Hitler's accommodation in the 'Führerbunker'. Snoring loudly, their legs stretched out in front of them, the three of them were lying harmoniously together, wrapped in woollen blankets in deep arm-chairs, which had been pushed in front of the bench along the right-hand wall. Only a few paces away, at the table opposite, sat Hitler and Goebbels, and on the bench along the left-hand wall sat Eva Braun. When Hitler saw me coming, he got up. It was not easy for him or for me to climb over the outstretched legs without waking the trio from their deep sleep. Goebbels, who followed us into the conference room, took particular care not to disturb them, which in view of his limp, appeared almost grotesque. Eva Braun could not resist a smile at this sight.

During the night of 27 April, after all verbal communications had been totally dislocated for a time, we had managed to establish a telephone link between Armed Forces High Command in Fürstenberg and the Reich Chancellery. But from 5 o'clock in the morning this link with the outside world was once again completely cut off. News about the situation of the troops fighting in areas outside Berlin therefore became increasingly scarce. The only sources of information about the situation which Bernd and I now had left were the transmitter and receiver operated by Lorenz, and the radio station of General Weidling's Fifty-Sixth Corps, which also served as the radio station for the Battle Commandant of Berlin. In the Reich Chancellery itself we no longer had any kind of mechanical means of communication.

When Hitler had personally asked Armed Forces High Command, via the Propaganda Ministry radio link, what had become of the relief attacks by Steiner's battle group in the north and Holste's corps in the west of Berlin, High Command had been unable to give any precise details and had evaded the question. In fact, the reports from the Ninth Army were quite devoid of hope. Attacking to the west from Frankfurt an der Oder, they had not got beyond the line Zossen–Baruth – to the south of Berlin. Squashed into the tiniest space with a vast mass of refugees, attacked on all sides by an overwhelmingly superior enemy, with hardly any vehicles and ammunition left, and no medical supplies for an army of wounded, the Ninth Army did not even remotely have the strength to continue their attack to the west. Hitler had issued the authorization for them to withdraw from the Oder Front, simultaneously initiating an attack to the west, at least three to five days too late. In Mecklenburg Marshall Rokossovsky's troops had reached the line Neustrelitz to Neubrandenburg to Anklam, and were preparing to push this spearhead farther westwards.

It was becoming increasingly apparent that there was a danger of the Berlin pocket being split in half. Because of the Red Army's attacks on the city from the north and south the narrowest section of the pocket was west of the *Tiergarten*. As a result there was a threat of an eastern pocket developing north of the line Frankfurter Allee–Alexanderplatz–Hallesches Tor–Landwehr Canal comprising the city centre district and parts of the precincts Friedrichshain and Prenzlauer Berg, and a western pocket grouped basically around the Wilmersdorf district, with a narrow link to the battle area held and defended by the Hitler Youth around the Pickelsdorf bridges over the Havel and including the Reich Sports Fields. There was also yet another pocket, held by the Twentieth Motorized Division, between Wannsee lake and Potsdam, which included the Pfaueninsel. There was no longer any link between this pocket and the weak, encircled corps commanded by General Reimann in the Potsdam area. This corps had made contact today, 28 April, with the Twentieth Corps of Wenck's Army on the narrow part of the lake at Alt-Geltow, to the south-east of Werder.

During my report on the situation in Berlin, to which Hitler had listened in silence, the intense Russian bombardment of the government district raged incessantly on. When several very heavy shells had landed in the precincts of the Reich Chancellery, and heavy lumps of concrete crashed down on to the lowest level of concrete above the bunker, probably a direct hit, Hitler put his shaking left hand on my forearm and interrupted my report. Leaning on the arm of the chair, he swivelled slowly round on his seat and half turned towards me. Then he gave me an indescribable look and asked: 'What do you think, what calibre gun are they firing out there? Could it penetrate right through down to here? You have been a soldier at the front, you must surely know?' I replied that it was most likely a 17.5 calibre, the calibre of the Russian heavy artillery, and that in my view the calibre and penetration were insufficient to destroy this bunker. Hitler seemed to be satisfied with my answer and allowed me to go on with my report.

On the way back from the conference we met SS Lieutenant-Colonel Fegelein escorted by two armed soldiers of the Escort Detachment. His epaulettes and collar flashes had been torn off; I could scarcely believe that this Hermann Fegelein, pale and dejected, was the same man I had so often seen during the past weeks. He had somehow managed to steal out of the Reich Chancellery unnoticed on 26 April. But on the following day Hitler had spotted that Fegelein, Himmler's representative, was missing from our number. He was suspicious at once, and sent out officers of his Escort Detachment in a search party. Sure enough they found him, in civilian clothes, in his own home in Charlottenburg. When Fegelein was brought in Hitler's disciples were beside themselves with rage and indignation that such a high official should have deserted, and he was reduced to the ranks at once. When I saw him he had spent the last twenty-four hours in an improvised cell, and was being taken to Hitler's bunker to be interrogated.

At about 6 o'clock we were ordered yet again to attend a conference with Hitler, though I had scarcely anything to add to what I had reported at midday. However it seemed that

Bernd had got hold of some very important news from Lorenz's and General Weidling's radios. The conference was unusually well attended for these days; the company included Goebbels, Burgdorf, Krebs, Admiral Voss and most of the liaison officers.

The news of the Ninth Army once again demonstrated, this time beyond any doubt, that they were on the verge of annihilation. Clearly, they were no longer capable of attacking a superior foe and capturing the twenty-five or thirty kilometres still separating them from Wenck's army. The Twentieth Corps of the Twelfth Army had held on to the territory they had gained, which was bounded roughly on the front facing the Ninth Army) by the line Miemegk–Beelitz–Ferch; but General Wenck was in no position to press his attack any farther in the direction of Berlin or to meet the Ninth Army. The Twentieth Corps on the right of the Twelfth Army was engaged in such fierce defensive fighting in this area that a continuation of the attack was inconceivable. To the left the Forty-First Corps of this Army under General Holste, was holding a very extended and relatively thinly-manned front, with absolutely no forces in reserve to the rear: moreover they were being incessantly attacked by Zhukov's armoured formations. Here too it was complete fantasy to think of an attack in the direction of Berlin: the commanders here were grateful enough if the front merely held.

Steiner's battle group, under the command of General von Tippelskirch's newly formed Twenty-First Army Group, had held the northern bank of the Ruppin Canal and the small bridgehead over it, in the face of an adversary ten or fifteen times stronger; but with the forces at present available it was too weak to gain even a few more metres of ground towards Berlin. The Twenty-Fifth *Panzer* Grenadier Division

168

and the Seventh Armoured Division had had to be withdrawn from the Twenty-First Army Group and from their position on the former right wing of the Third Tank Army near Oranienburg so that they could block the advancing spearheads of Marshal Rokossovsky's forces. Rokossovsky was about to attack farther westwards across the line Neustrelitz to Neubrandenburg. Thus even for Hitler, the last possible hope of launching a relief attack on Berlin disappeared. Nothing new had emerged from this meeting that any realistic member of the company did not already know; but, even so, these completely undisguised facts, quite devoid of hope, had a very depressing effect on us all, Hitler included. The one moment of relief came when the almost incredible news arrived of the safe landing of a replacement aircraft for Ritter von Greim. It was an Arado-type training plane, and it was immediately got under cover for fear of shelling.

Much later, about 7 o'clock, Lorenz came hurrying over from the Propaganda Ministry during a break in the firing with another sensational piece of news. He had picked up a BBC London newscast in which there had been a Reuter report that SS *Reichsführer* Heinrich Himmler had offered the Allies an unconditional surrender on behalf of all the German troops. In fact, as we subsequently learned, these negotiations had been conducted during the previous five days through the Swedish Count Bernadotte, in the Swedish Consulate in Lübeck.

This news upset Hitler far more than the alleged defection or even treachery of Hermann Göring. Göring's radio message had, at least, acknowledged Hitler's authority to some extent. Himmler, on the other hand had totally ignored his 'Führer' and acted completely independently over the most important issue of all. Moreover, Hitler had always thought of Himmler as his most loyal and devoted supporter and political ally. The last mainstay of whatever faith he may have had left in the loyalty and goodwill of his supporters now collapsed. He succumbed to a helpless paroxysm of rage, full of hate and contempt, such as few human beings can have experienced. He described Himmler's deceitful negotiations as the most shameful betrayal in human history.

When he had calmed down somewhat he withdrew into the conference room with Bormann and Goebbels for a lengthy discussion, during which the rest of us waited in the anteroom. When he reappeared he ordered that Fegelein be brought before him and subjected to a rigorous interrogation on the subject of Himmler's activities. As it fell out, Fegelein yielded no information of any significance, but, although there was no proof whatsoever of his complicity in the Himmler plot, Hitler ordered him to be shot at once in the garden of the Reich Chancellery, and the sentence was carried out forthwith. Hitler received the news of Fegelein's execution in a state of pathological excitement. He rushed immediately to see Field-Marshal Ritter von Greim, who was still lying on a stretcher, and ordered him to leave the Reich Chancellery and Berlin right away for Schleswig-Holstein, and to put Himmler under arrest. He gave these orders in a voice charged with uncontrolled hysteria, making it quite clear that Greim's best course would be to liquidate Himmler without delay. Both Greim and Hanna Reitsch insisted that they wanted to stick it out in the bunker (presumably out of some sense of loyalty), but they could not make Hitler alter his decision. They were driven in an armed vehicle from the Reich Chancellery to the plane, and, to our general amazement they achieved a successful take-off in well-nigh impossible conditions, going on to fly safely over Berlin, through the dense Russian anti-aircraft fire. Ritter von Greim and Hanna Reitsch landed, unharmed, in

Rochlin, in Mecklenberg, on the night of 28 April.

One can only conjecture whether it was due to Ritter von Greim's successful take-off or merely the exhaustion which sets in after two hours of a state of excitement near to frenzy, but at any rate Hitler now quietened down again completely. Without a word to his entourage, his face an expressionless mask, he withdrew into his living quarters. Not so the ever-alert Martin Bormann. That very evening he radioed a message to Dönitz at his Staff Quarters 'Pike' near Plön, in which he openly accused the leaders of the Armed Forces High Command (i.e. Keitel and Jodl) of treachery, for their failure to push the troops hard enough for the relief of Berlin to become a reality. He closed with the words: 'The Chancellery is already a heap of debris!' The message was typical of Bormann's behaviour, as was the method by which he chose to send it, going the long way round via Admiral von Puttkamer in Berchtesgaden because he did not trust the *Wehrmacht* High Command. None of them – Bormann, Hitler, Goebbels or the rest – would have it that the German Army was finally drained of strength; nor would they ever admit to themselves or those around them that the enemy was many times stronger than they were. The way they looked at it, any failure must be the result of treachery.

Bernd woke me up as morning broke on 29 April. He was already sitting at his desk working, and it was some minutes before he looked up and said, quite casually, 'Our Führer got married last night, Gerhard.' He burst into laughter at my baffled face, and I readily joined in. At this the resolute voice of General Krebs boomed out from behind the curtain dividing the room: 'Have you taken leave of your senses, gentlemen, laughing so disrespectfully at the sovereign leader of your country?' Bernd waited until Krebs left the room and then he told me what had taken place the night before.

It seemed barely credible, but that night there had been a proper wedding, with registrars, a loud and clear, 'I do', witnesses, and a wedding breakfast. The usual formalities of a civil marriage were carried out by an official of the Propaganda Ministry. Goebbels and Martin Bormann were the witnesses. The guests at the meal and the short celebration which followed were General Krebs, General Burgdorf, Goebbels and his wife, Bormann, Hitler's secretaries and his cook, Fräulein Manzialy.

Later Hitler had left the little wedding party with his private secretary, Frau Gertrud Junge, in order to dictate to her his Political Testament and his private will, naming Bormann as executor. Bernd had also managed to discover that arrangements had been made for copies of these wills to be taken out of Berlin and delivered to Admiral Dönitz who was chosen to be Hitler's successor, and to Field-Marshal Schörner, the Supreme Commander of the Army Group fighting in Bohemia. The messengers selected were Hitler's Army adjutant, Major Johannmeier, Bormann's right-hand man, SS *Standartenführer* Zander, and Heinz Lorenz from the Propaganda Ministry.

When Bernd's tale was over we went back to our work, co-ordinating the scanty morning reports. Outside, the battle for the city centre raged on with undiminished violence. The intense Russian bombardment rained down almost incessantly on the government district and the Russian attack drew ever relentlessly nearer. At about 9 o'clock the hurricane of artillery fire suddenly stopped, and shortly afterwards our runners reported that the Russians were advancing with tanks and infantry towards the Wilhelmplatz. It grew quite silent in the bunker. Everyone held his breath and listened in a state of tension that had increased to an almost intolerable pitch. At last, after an hour, another

172

runner reported that the Russians had come to a halt about four to five hundred metres from the Reich Chancellery.

Into the midst of this tension came a fresh report with news from General Weidling's staff that the link between General Reimann's encircled corps in the Potsdam area and the Twelfth Army to the south-east of Werder was still intact. In this piece of news Bernd and I saw our chance. Whenever we two had been alone over the past few days our conversation had had one recurrent theme – how to get sent out of the bunker on some combat mission.

When Krebs arrived a short while later, we were ready for him with our maps and papers and he asked for a summary of the situation that morning. I mentioned the fighting on the Belle-Alliance Platz and in the Potsdamer Strasse and the strenuous efforts of our troops to hold the Russians at bay between the Kantstrasse and Bismarckstrasse. All the other news was confused and contradictory. Then the Major reported on the situation of Wenck's Army and Reimann's corps mentioning the link which still existed between the two units to the south-east of Werder. This was the moment Bernd had been waiting for to bring up our idea. He explained to the General how useful it would be if we two were to make speedy contact with the Twelfth Army and put Wenck completely in the picture about the true situation in Berlin and the Reich Chancellery. He insisted that as well as urging General Wenck to hurry we could also act as guides for his attack on Berlin. I supported these arguments as best I could, pointing out that there was hardly anything left for us to do in the bunker. Krebs could not bring himself to make a decision in case he should get into trouble with Hitler, but General Burgdorf, who joined us shortly afterwards, was remarkably easy to convince and became quite enthusiastic about our mission. His adjutant, Lieutenant-Colonel Weiss, decided that he would accompany us. Bormann, too, provided some quite unexpected support, and together he and Burgdorf succeeded in persuading Krebs of the necessity for our journey and for him to broach the subject with Hitler at the next conference.

About 12 o'clock Hitler summoned the midday conference, which included Bormann, Burgdorf and Goebbels. Krebs was to read the report, but there were only the most sketchy of maps for him to go on. The city centre was the one place where the situation was still reasonably clear. Otherwise our picture of the fighting in the Berlin pocket was completely confused by rumours, supposition and contradictory reports.

Krebs intended to try to win Hitler's support for our enterprise directly after the conference. The most nerve-racking moment of my whole life had arrived. Krebs came to the end of his report and then he added quite casually that three young officers wanted to try to break out of Berlin to make contact with General Wenck and enlighten him about the situation in Berlin and in the Reich Chancellery, and to urge him to hurry. Hitler looked up from the map and gazed absently straight ahead. After a silence lasting several seconds he asked, 'Who are these officers?' Krebs told him our names. 'Who are they and where are they now?' Burgdorf answered and gave him the desired information in some detail. More minutes of unbelievable tension went by, seconds which seemed to us an eternity. Freytag looked across at me and I knew that his nerves were as strained as mine. Suddenly Hitler looked me in the face and said: 'How are you planning to get out of Berlin?'

I stepped up to the table and explained our plan to him on the map: along the *Tiergarten*, then the Zoo station, Joachimstaler Strasse, Kurfürstendamm – Adolf Hitler-Platz – the Stadium – the bridges at Pichelsdorf. From there

174

along the Havel in a rowing boat, between the Russian lines as far as Wannsee lake.

Hitler interrupted me: 'Bormann, supply these three officers with an electric motor-boat, otherwise they'll never get through.' I felt the blood rushing to my head. Was this idiotic motor-boat going to ruin the entire plan? Where in the world was Bormann going to find such a thing in our present state of affairs? Before Bormann could answer I pulled myself together and turned to Hitler: 'Führer, we will get hold of a motor-boat ourselves and deaden the noise. I'm convinced that we will get through.' To our intense relief Hitler was satisfied. He slowly got up, looked at me wearily, shook hands with each of us and said: 'Give my regards to Wenck. Tell him to hurry or it will be too late.'

Passes for crossing the German lines had been made out in advance, and now Burgdorf handed one to each of us. Then, at last, we were able to leave the room and, once outside in the passage, we shook hands joyfully. Once again we had a fighting chance, albeit a very slim one. We no longer faced the prospect of that everlasting waiting in the bunker. It was now 12.45. We got ready for our journey in tearing haste, packing plenty of rations, donning camouflage jackets and steel helmets. Finally we slung sub-machine-guns over our shoulders and collected our indispensable maps. Freytag removed the red stripe from his trousers, and we shook hands quickly. We made our brief farewells and departed. It was 1.30 in the afternoon of 29 April.

7. ESCAPE FROM BERLIN AND HOMECOMING*

Ducking down against the wall of the bunker exit leading on to Hermann-Göring-Strasse, we held back for a few minutes to shelter from a mortar attack. From somewhere, a burst of machine-gun fire whistled over our heads, the bullets embedding themselves in the walls above us. Thick black smoke rolled towards us from the direction of the Potsdamer Platz. Then we pressed on, past mortar craters, shot-up vehicles and dead soldiers and civilians, across Hermann-Göring-Strasse into the *Tiergarten*. We were out of the worst artillery fire here, in the middle of the housing blocks. Then suddenly six, eight, ten Russian dive-bombers came shrieking straight for us. With a leap we took cover in a house entrance. Outside, bombs were falling, aircraft cannon chattering. Here in the hallway people lay and sat around, women in despair, terrified children and defeated soldiers. From one corner came the groaning of the wounded. We raced on. Next to a mortar crater lay nine or ten dead civilians, some of them mutilated beyond recognition – But keep going! A smell of decomposition everywhere, the occasional dead horse, knocked-out vehicles, more burning houses. We crawled, climbed, stumbled our way forward, making steady progress towards the west. In one or two front gardens we

---

*In the following pages Gerhardt Boldt departs from the role of eyewitness which was his reason for writing this book. But the description which follows is an integral part of his personal story. On 29 April 1945, shortly before Hitler's death, the German surrender, and the final victory of the Red Army in Berlin, Boldt succeeded in escaping from the conquered city.

176

came across German gun-emplacements still intact, ten or fifteen of them. They belonged to the artillery of the Fifty-Sixth Tank Corps. They had been silent for days: the ammunition was finished.

So it went on, for the four hours it took us to cover a distance which would normally have been a half-hour walk, until shortly before 6 pm, when we reached the underground shelter at the Zoo station to snatch thirty minutes' rest. With the infantry battle unmistakably getting nearer every minute, the scene here was again one of huddled, terrified, despairing humanity. In complete darkness we passed through flattened houses and courtyards to reach Joachim Strasse – Kurfürstendamm and Adolf Hitler-Platz. The first Russian tanks had already passed through this spot on that same afternoon, 29 April. From a Hitler Youth Leader in command there we obtained the services of a lad to drive us through partly occupied territory to the Reich Stadium, where another small combat group was holding out. With unbelievable skill the boy piloted us at break-neck speed through the western sector of Charlottenburg. Scarcely half an hour later our footsteps were echoing through the vast amphitheatre of the Olympic Stadium. Not a soul was in sight. The wan moonlight lent the still undamaged building an eerie magic. ... We spent a few hours of the night with a small Hitler Youth unit in rooms at the western exit of the stadium, and at first light set out from the Reich Sports Field towards the Havel bridges at Pichelsdorf. Our small group, strengthened by the addition of a few soldiers, was large enough for self-defence in an emergency. Colonel von Below had also joined us: he had left the Reich Chancellery some hours after us with a message for Field-Marshal Keitel.

Hitler Youth fighters, armed with anti-tank mortars, were lying, singly or in pairs, scattered among the trenches and foxholes in front of the Pichelsdorf Bridge, on both sides of the Heerstrasse. The light of dawn was already strong enough to reveal distinctly the dark silhouettes of heavy Russian tanks on the Heerstrasse, standing out from the murky background. They were about a kilometre away in the direction of the Heerstrasse station, and their guns were trained on the bridges. In groups of three we rushed at full pelt, lungs bursting, across the long bridge and collapsed gasping on the other side, profoundly thankful for the protective slope of the road. A fighting group was holding out in the little wood alongside the road, and after a long search we found the commander Chief Area Leader – *Obergebietsführer* – Schlünder, in a timber-shored dug-out in the slope of a small hollow. After establishing our identities he told us about the fate of his troops: 'When the fighting started here five days ago, we numbered about 5,000 Hitler Youth. There were a few soldiers with us but we faced impossible odds. The boys were equipped with nothing but their rifles and mortars; they were complete greenhorns, and in withering artillery fire, which they had never before experienced, they were decimated. No reserves or relief arrived to allow the lads to snatch even a brief spell of sleep.' We went outside and Schlünder added bitterly, 'The worst time for my boys is at night, when it's quiet, having to listen to the desperate cries of women and girls over there.' Schlünder seemed very perplexed and was obviously racked by doubts, but nevertheless Hitler's orders kept him and his boys at their stations by the bridges. These murderous, criminal orders had pressed weapons into the hands of untrained children and thrown them to the mercy of forces whose crushing superiority made their destruction a certainty.

On 1 May, shortly after midnight, we pushed off in a collapsible canoe from the island which forms a small spit of land between the two arms of the Havel near Pichelsdorf. We were aiming for Wannsee lake, about ten kilometres away, beyond Russian-occupied territory. According to our information of the previous day, a small German force of the Twentieth Motorized Infantry Division was supposed to be still holding out there. I sat at the prow, ready to open up with my tommy-gun; behind me were Lieutenant-Colonel Weiss and then Bernd, who were both paddling. At first we elected to stay in mid-stream on the wide Havel, but when, as we drew level with the Kaiser Wilhelm monument, we caught sight of a Russian boat-trap, we fled into the sheltering darkness of the west bank. The night was starlit and cool. Near Kladow we were so close to the shore that we could distinctly hear Russian voices, the deep throb of engines running and other clattering noises. We passed Schwanenwerder at about 2.45 am. The laughter and whooping of Russian officers drunk with victory rang out from the brightly lit villas. Just beyond Schwanenwerder our heavily-laden canoe was nearly swamped by a stiff breeze that blew up from the Great Wannsee lake. In the first light of 1 May we landed on the Wannsee peninsula opposite Schwanenwerder. On landing we were stunned to notice, somewhat belatedly, a well-camouflaged anti-tank gun trained on our boat.

The group fighting here had already planned a break-out from their beleaguered position for the night of 1 May, hoping to join up with Wenck's army south of Potsdam. Reporting to the command post we were heartily welcomed by Majors Meier, Zander and Lorenz, who had left the Reich Chancellery before us. They and Colonel von Below intended to land somewhere between Kladow and Gatow and trek towards the west from there. We, however, joined the division, since our mission was clearly tied up with Wenck's Army.

The break-out on the night of 1 May was ill-starred from

the beginning. Disaster occurred at a six-foot tank barrier, where there was a viaduct leading to the bridge connecting Great and Little Wannsee. The bulk of the troops attempting the break-through were simply gunned down. Countless dead and wounded lay piled in great heaps in the very confined space on and around the half-destroyed bridge. The few men who got through to establish a bridgehead on the other side, were massacred in an immediate Russian counter-attack. Lieutenant-Colonel Weiss was captured: Bernd and I went to earth in a pine-thicket. Before nightfall we had dug ourselves in with hands and feet into the loose forest soil and covered ourselves with dead leaves: our luck was in, for the Russians, despite scouring that stretch of woodland all day, failed to unearth us.

At dawn on 3 May we divested ourselves of our uniforms, exchanging them for old, torn, civilian clothes. And then, on that same day we heard that the battle for Berlin was over and that Hitler was dead. The news obviously relieved us of our mission, and so we set off right away to trek to the south-west. Our immediate goal was the Elbe crossing at Wittenberg. The route we selected went through Teltow and then across the Army training grounds at Jüterbog; we assumed that the Russians would prefer to concentrate on thickly populated centres rather than deserted training grounds. The stream of foreign workers whom we encountered straggling westwards gave us the idea of trying to pass ourselves off as workers from Luxemburg. We both spoke French well enough to feel reasonably safe in this role.

About noon we had an extremely disconcerting experience. Bernd and I were leaning over the parapet of a bridge across the *Autobahn*, running a professional eye over the Russian troops pouring in two endless columns along the motorway towards the west. We were so deep in our conversation and in our thoughts that we did not hear a Russian army lorry pulling up directly behind us. A Russian officer tapped me on the shoulder and, in broken German, asked me the way. In even worse German, with a French accent, I gave him the information he required. We watched with relief as the lorry drove off. A greater shock was in store for us, however, for there, in the lorry, with a dozen other captured German soldiers, sat Lieutenant-Colonel Weiss, whom we had lost sight of in the break-out at Wannsee.

Next day we arrived at the narrows of Blankensee Lake and spent the night in a small hunting cabin. About one in the morning we were awakened by a lot of shouting. Electric torches were shone into our eyes: rifles poked through the window-panes pointed unmistakably at us. A Russian patrol! But so well did we play our parts as homeward-bound foreign workers that after a short exchange the Russians moved on and left us in peace.

The sun was already low in the sky, and we had just passed a deserted village on the Army training grounds at Jüterbog, when suddenly a Russian army truck rounded the corner and squealed to a halt in front of us. In a second, a dozen Russian soldiers with a Commissar at their head had jumped down and surrounded us, the muzzles of their tommy-guns covering us menacingly. Putting up a great show of indignation we rejected all charges of being 'Germanski soldier'; we swore violently, with a flood of French expletives and much gesticulating, that we had nothing whatever to do with the Germanski. They did not seem entirely convinced, however, for after an initial hesitation they began to 'frisk' these 'French civilians'. In the process they brought to light army watches, rings, compasses, chocolate, an amulet and, unfortunately, our General Staff maps! The evidence against us was overwhelming. The Commissar waved the maps and compasses excitedly round, repeatedly shouting 'Germanski soldier'. In the end he abruptly told us to sit down, and we feared the worst. But we got off lightly because the Commissar only had his eye on our boots! While one man was obeying his order to remove our footwear, a fierce and noisy squabble broke out among the rest of the squad for possession of our other effects. The quarrel became more and more lively, and luckily for us, the Commissar himself became involved. We seemed to be completely forgotten in the fracas. At this point a pleasant-looking, older Russian stepped up to us and motioned with his thumb. His meaning was unmistakable. We instantly took to our heels, and in our stockinged feet made a successful silent escape around the nearest corner.

The next day, near Marzahana, at a road sign saying 'Wittenberg 18 kilometres', we again ran straight into a Russian road check that was hidden round a blind bend. We were marshalled towards a group of sixty or seventy French, Dutch and Belgians and delivered with them to a transit camp for foreign workers, eight kilometres down the road. Ironically enough, fate had decreed that all who styled themselves as Germans were being allowed by the Russians to go on their way scot free!

Once in the camp we were registered, and soon learned that we were to be transported to the west in American lorries. We preferred to decamp the same night, and reached Wittenberg without further incident twenty-four hours later. We spent the next few days in vain attempts to cross the Elbe unobserved. We finally performed the crossing one misty morning, at a point some five kilometres downstream from Wittenberg. Eventually, we landed up in a Russian encampment near Oranienbaum, in the area between the Elbe and the Mulde, once again unwilling guests of the Red Army. On another occasion, when we had almost brought off the swim across the Mulde, the current turned out to be too strong for me. I was rather under the weather at the time, and we had to give up. Finally we succeeded at noon on 11 May, north of Raguhn. Safe on the other side, we threw ourselves on to the grass, exhausted but overjoyed: we were on American-occupied soil at last.

Next morning at 5 o'clock Bernd and I sadly took leave of each other, he to push on southwards towards Leipzig, I to strike off northwards for Lübeck. In these past few weeks we had become firm friends, and now a terrible but unforgettable period of our lives was behind us.

I had to trek for nearly two more weeks before the final homecoming to my wife and child at the end of May. Early in 1946 I was arrested by the British, and went from an interrogation camp to an internment camp, where the first drafts of this account were written.

POSTSCRIPT – A LAST ECHO*
Hitler's Death – The End in the Reich Chancellery –
The Surrender of Berlin

On 29 and 30 April the military situation in beleaguered Berlin greatly deteriorated. Late on the twenty-ninth General Weidling, commanding the defence of the city, again put to Hitler the idea of a concerted effort to break through and join Wenck's army at Potsdam. Hitler once again refused. On 30 April between 3 and 4 pm, in his private suite in the Reich Chancellery bunker, Adolf Hitler shot himself. His wife Eva, née Braun, ended her life at the same time by taking poison. The bodies were carried out, wrapped in blankets, to the Reich Chancellery garden, soaked in about fifty gallons of petrol, and burnt.

Acting on Goebbels' orders, General Krebs that night opened negotiations with the Red Army commander in Berlin, Marshal Zhukov, for a complete end to the fighting in the city. Though tedious and protracted, the talks led to no positive result.

It was not until exactly twenty-four hours after the event that Hitler's successor designate, Admiral Dönitz, was informed over the radio by Goebbels and Bormann of the Führer's death. Goebbels reached the end of the road when it was finally clear that the cease-fire negotiations had broken down. During the afternoon of 1 May he poisoned his five

*Using historical documents, this chapter outlines the fate of people and army groups mentioned earlier.

184

children. A few hours later, between 8 and 9 pm, Goebbels and his wife had themselves shot by an SS sentry in the garden of the Reich Chancellery. Goebbels' adjutant, SS *Hauptsturmführer* Schwagermann, was entrusted with the last duty of soaking their bodies in petrol and setting light to them.

Meanwhile preparations were being completed in the Reich Chancellery for all remaining personnel to make an all-out attempt out towards the west, commanded by Mohnke and Bormann. Towards 10 pm they struck out in three separate groups from the Reich Chancellery, proceeding by way of underground railway tunnels from the Wilhelmplatz towards the Friedrichstrasse Station–Weidendamm Bridge area, where the breakthrough was launched with tank support. This concerted attempt failed; only a few stragglers got through to the west; Bormann and Dr Stumpfegger according to Axmann's evidence (admittedly unconfirmed), are said to have been killed. The diplomat Hewel likewise died in the attempt. Mohnke remained in Russian captivity until 1956. Generals Krebs and Burgdorf did not take part. They both committed suicide.

On the night of 1 May the Commander-in-Chief in Berlin, General Weidling, successfully negotiated surrender terms with Marshal Zhukov for all troops fighting in the city. Immediately afterwards General Weidling was captured by the Russians and removed. This capitulation was supposed to bring about a complete armistice by 2 May. General resistance certainly ceased, but there were still small groups fighting on without any unifying command. On 2 and 3 May several concerted efforts to break out were undertaken by various army units, who would have done anything to avoid Russian captivity. By 4 May the cease-fire in Berlin was complete.

The End of Army High Command and
of the Dönitz Government

As we have already seen, Army High Command had been transferred on 22 April 1945 to Krampnitz near Potsdam, but with the approach of Russian tanks these headquarters were abandoned the very next day, when the High Command moved on to Fürstenberg, about seventy kilometres north of Berlin. Here a stand was made until 29 April, when Russian troops were immediately outside Fürstenberg. The next move was to Dobbin in South Mecklenburg. The High Command's main concern from 22 April to 1 May was the relief of Berlin; Keitel and Jodl in particular made great personal efforts to that end. During this time Keitel was almost constantly to be found at one or other of the command posts of the armies, army corps and divisions that were earmarked for the relief attack. On 1 May, by order of the new Head of State, Admiral Dönitz, High Command was moved via Wismar, to Plön in Holstein, where Dönitz had set up his staff quarters. Then, when Dönitz moved the seat of his new government to Flensburg-Mürwick, High Command went with him.

On 2 May Dönitz initiated the first tentative discussions about a surrender in the north-German area. Admiral von Friedeburg and Field-Marshal Montgomery were the negotiators. The first signature was set to a general surrender by Jodl on 7 May at 2.41 am in Reims, at Eisenhower's headquarters. The cease-fire on all fronts was to run from midnight on 9 May.

In order to gain time, Admiral Dönitz quite deliberately – and to some extent successfully – tried to delay the conclusion of the armistice and surrender agreement. His reasons were as follows:

1. The withdrawal of troops and refugees from Curland and the Vistula delta was going ahead at full speed, using every available inch of shipboard space. It was important to gain time for this operation.

2. It was equally important to play for time to facilitate the retreat of Army Group Vistula in Mecklenburg. In their westward progress the two armies of this group, the Third Tank Army and the Twenty-First Army, were sweeping before them a vast flood of refugees from Pomerania, Mecklenburg and Stettin. When on 5 May the British accepted the north-German surrender from Dönitz, the British and American forces stood along a line running from Ludwigslust through Schwerin to Wismar. Dönitz tried to get as many refugees and troops behind this line as possible, and had a large measure of success.

3. A race for time was also going on in the case of the 1,200,000 strong Central Army Group under Field-Marshal Schörner in Bohemia. The massed forces of the Fourth Tank Army, the Seventeenth Army and the First Tank Army still stood, on 6 May, in the Riesengebirge area, roughly on a line from Görlitz to Glatz, westward of Mährisch, Ostrau and Brünn. The distance from the American front line, which had been pushed forward to a line Karlsbad–Pilsen–Passau, was, at some points, as much as 250 kilometres. On top of this came the Czech uprising in Bohemia and Moravia. The Commander-in-Chief of the Army Group, Field-Marshal F. Schörner (named in Hitler's 'testament' as the new Chief of the General Staff) abandoned his troops when their situation was most desperate, to secure his own personal safety.

On 9 May 1945 at 4 pm in Berlin-Karlshorst, the capitulation of all the German Armed Forces to the Allies was confirmed by the signatures of Field-Marshal Keitel, Admiral von Friedeburg and General Stumpf. It came into effect immediately.

On 23 May 1945 Dönitz's government, together with the Army Staffs, were arrested and imprisoned.

Field-Marshal Keitel and Generals Jodl and Kaltenbrunner were sentenced to death by the Allied Military Tribunal at Nuremberg and executed by hanging.